# Quick & Easy
# Pasta

*p*

# Contents

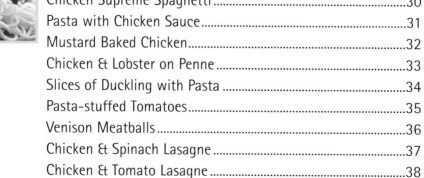

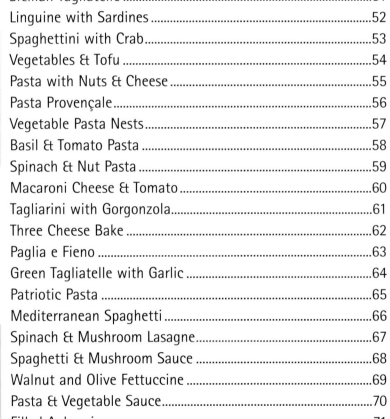

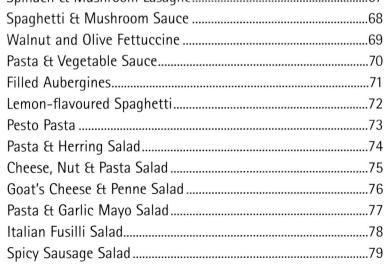

# Introduction

**Pasta has existed in one form or another since the days of the Roman Empire and remains one of the most versatile ingredients in the kitchen. It can be combined with almost anything from meat to fish, vegetables to fruit, and is even delicious served with simple herb sauces. No storecupboard should be without a supply of dried pasta, which, combined with a few other stock ingredients, can be turned into a mouthwatering and nutritious meal within minutes.**

## Why eat pasta?
Most pasta is made from durum wheat flour and contains protein and carbohydrates. It is a good source of slow-release energy and has the additional advantage of being value for money.

## Varieties
There is an enormous range of different types of pasta, some of which are listed on the opposite page. Many are available both dried and fresh. Unless you have access to a good Italian delicatessen, it is probably not worth buying fresh, unfilled pasta, but even supermarkets sell high-quality tortellini, capelletti, ravioli and agnolotti. Best of all is to make fresh pasta at home. It takes a little time, but is quite easy and well worth the effort. You can mix the dough by hand or prepare it in a food processor if you prefer.

## Colours and flavours
Pasta may be coloured and flavoured with extra ingredients that are usually added with the beaten egg:
Black:   add 1 tsp squid or cuttlefish ink.
Green:   add 115 g/4 oz well-drained cooked spinach when kneading.
Purple:  work 1 large, cooked beetroot in a food processor and add with an extra 60 g/2 oz flour.
Red:     add 2 tbsp tomato purée.

## Cooking pasta
Always use a large saucepan for cooking pasta and bring lightly salted water to the boil. Add the pasta and 1 tbsp olive oil, but do not cover or the water will boil over. Quickly bring the water back to a rolling boil and avoid overcooking. When the pasta is tender, but still firm to

the bite, drain and toss with butter, olive oil or your prepared sauce and serve as soon as possible.

The cooking times given here are guidelines only:

Fresh unfilled pasta:    2–3 minutes
Fresh filled pasta:      8–10 minutes
Dried unfilled pasta:    10–12 minutes
Dried filled pasta:      15–20 minutes

## Basic Pasta Dough
If you wish to make your own pasta for the dishes in this book, follow this simple recipe.

### SERVES 4
#### INGREDIENTS

450 g/1 lb durum wheat flour

4 eggs, lightly beaten

1 tbsp olive oil

salt

**1** Lightly flour a work surface. Sift the flour with a pinch of salt into a mound. Make a well in the centre and add the eggs and olive oil.

**2** Using a fork or your fingertips, gradually work the mixture until the ingredients are combined. Knead vigorously for 10–15 minutes.

**3** Set the dough aside to rest for 25 minutes, before rolling it out as thinly and evenly as possible and using as desired.

## Types of pasta

There are as many as 200 different pasta shapes and about three times as many names for them. New shapes are being designed – and named – all the time and the same shape may be called a different name in different regions of Italy.

anelli, anellini: *small rings for soup*

bucatini: *long, medium-thick tubes*

cannelloni: *large, thick, round pasta tubes*

capelli d'angelo: *thin strands of 'angel hair'*

conchiglie: *ridged shells*

conchigliette: *little shells*

cresti di gallo: *curved-shaped*

ditali, ditalini: *short tubes*

eliche: *loose spirals*

farfalle: *bows*

fettuccine: *medium ribbons*

fusilli: *spirals*

gemelli: *two pieces wrapped together as 'twins'*

lasagne: *flat, rectangular sheets*

linguine: *long, flat ribbons*

lumache: *snail-shaped shells*

lumaconi: *big shells*

macaroni: *long- or short-cut tubes*

orecchiette: *ear-shaped*

penne: *quill-shaped*

rigatoni: *thick, ridged tubes*

spaghetti: *fine or medium rods*

tagliarini: *thin ribbons*

tagliatelle: *broad ribbons*

vermicelli: *fine pasta, usually folded into skeins*

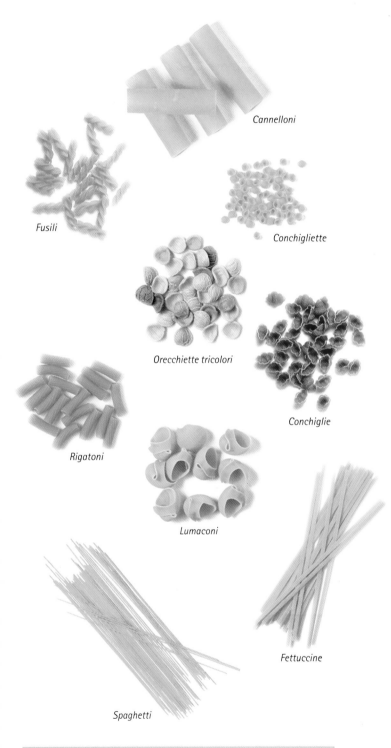

Cannelloni

Fusili

Conchigliette

Orecchiette tricolori

Conchiglie

Rigatoni

Lumaconi

Fettuccine

Spaghetti

| KEY | |
|-----|-----|
|  | Simplicity level 1–3 (1 easiest, 3 slightly harder) |
|  | Preparation time |
|  | Cooking time |

# Italian Cream of Tomato Soup

Plum tomatoes are ideal for making soups and sauces, as they have denser, less watery flesh than round varieties.

## NUTRITIONAL INFORMATION

| | | | |
|---|---|---|---|
| Calories | 555 | Sugars | 18g |
| Protein | 11g | Fat | 32g |
| Carbohydrate | 60g | Saturates | 19g |

15 mins          40 mins

### SERVES 4

## INGREDIENTS

4 tbsp unsalted butter

1 large onion, chopped

600 ml/1 pint vegetable stock

900 g/2 lb Italian plum tomatoes, skinned and roughly chopped

pinch of bicarbonate of soda

225 g/8 oz dried fusilli

1 tbsp caster sugar

150 ml/5 fl oz double cream

salt and pepper

fresh basil leaves, to garnish

deep-fried croûtons, to serve

1 Melt the unsalted butter in a large saucepan, add the chopped onion and fry for 3 minutes. Add 300 ml/10 fl oz of vegetable stock to the pan, and stir in the chopped tomatoes and bicarbonate of soda. Bring the mixture to the boil and simmer for 20 minutes.

2 Remove the pan from the heat and set aside to cool. Purée the soup in a blender or food processor and pour through a fine sieve back into the saucepan, pushing it through with a wooden spoon.

3 Add the remaining vegetable stock and the fusilli to the pan, and season to taste with salt and pepper.

4 Add the sugar to the pan, bring to the boil, then lower the heat and simmer for about 15 minutes.

5 Pour the soup into a warm tureen, swirl the double cream around the surface of the soup and garnish with fresh basil leaves. Serve the soup immediately with deep-fried croûtons.

## COOK'S TIP

To make tomato and carrot soup, use half the quantity of vegetable stock combined with the same amount of carrot juice and 175 g/6 oz grated carrot to the recipe, cooking the carrot with the onion.

# Lemon & Chicken Soup

This delicately flavoured summer soup is surprisingly easy to make, and tastes absolutely delicious.

## NUTRITIONAL INFORMATION

Calories ...... 506    Sugars ........ 4g
Protein ....... 19g    Fat .......... 31g
Carbohydrate .. 41g    Saturates ..... 19g

5–10 mins    1¼ hrs

### SERVES 4

## INGREDIENTS

6 tbsp butter

8 shallots, thinly sliced

2 carrots, thinly sliced

2 celery sticks, thinly sliced

225 g/8 oz boned chicken breasts, finely chopped

3 lemons

1.2 litres/2 pints chicken stock

225 g/8 oz dried spaghetti, broken into small pieces

150 ml/5 fl oz double cream

salt and white pepper

### TO GARNISH

fresh parsley sprig

3 lemon slices, halved

1 Melt the butter in a large saucepan. Add the shallots, carrots, celery and chicken and cook over a low heat, stirring occasionally, for 8 minutes.

2 Thinly pare the lemons, blanch the rind in boiling water for 3 minutes, and squeeze the juice from the lemons.

3 Add the blanched lemon rind and juice to the pan, together with the chicken stock. Bring the mixture slowly to the boil over a low heat and simmer for 40 minutes, stirring occasionally.

4 Add the spaghetti to the pan and cook for 15 minutes. Season to taste with salt and white pepper and add the cream. Heat through, but do not allow the soup to boil or it will curdle.

5 Pour the soup into a tureen or individual bowls. Garnish with the fresh parsley and the half slices of lemon and serve immediately.

## COOK'S TIP

You can prepare this soup up to the end of step 3 in advance, so that all you need do before serving is heat it through before adding the pasta and the finishing touches.

# Chicken & Sweetcorn Soup

This warming, creamy chicken soup is made into a meal in itself with the addition of strands of vermicelli.

## NUTRITIONAL INFORMATION

| | |
|---|---|
| Calories . . . . . . 457 | Sugars . . . . . . . . 3g |
| Protein . . . . . . . 16g | Fat . . . . . . . . . . 21g |
| Carbohydrate . . 36g | Saturates . . . . . 12g |

5 mins       30 mins

### SERVES 4

## I N G R E D I E N T S

450 g/1 lb boned chicken breasts,
  cut into strips

1.2 litres/2 pints chicken stock

150 ml/5 fl oz double cream

100 g/3½ oz dried vermicelli

1 tbsp cornflour

3 tbsp milk

175 g/6 oz sweetcorn kernels

salt and pepper

1 Put the chicken, stock and cream into a large pan and bring to the boil over a low heat. Reduce the heat slightly and simmer for about 20 minutes. Season the soup with salt and pepper to taste.

2 Meanwhile, cook the vermicelli in lightly salted boiling water for 10–12 minutes, until just tender. Drain the pasta and keep warm.

3 In a small bowl, mix together the cornflour and milk to make a smooth paste. Stir the cornflour mixture into the soup until it has thickened.

4 Add the sweetcorn and vermicelli to the pan and heat through.

5 Transfer the soup into a warm tureen or individual soup bowls and serve, immediately, while it is still hot.

### COOK'S TIP

If you are short of time, buy ready-cooked chicken, remove any skin and cut it into slices.

# Spaghetti alla Carbonara

Ensure that all of the cooked ingredients are as hot as possible before adding the eggs, so that they cook on contact.

## NUTRITIONAL INFORMATION

Calories ..... 1092  Sugars ........ 9g
Protein ....... 37g  Fat .......... 69g
Carbohydrate .. 86g  Saturates ..... 36g

 10 mins   5–10 mins

### SERVES 4

## INGREDIENTS

425 g/15 oz dried spaghetti

2 tbsp olive oil

1 large onion, thinly sliced

2 garlic cloves, chopped

175 g/6 oz rindless bacon, cut into thin strips

2 tbsp butter

175 g/6 oz mushrooms, thinly sliced

300 ml/10 fl oz double cream

3 eggs, beaten

100 g /3½ oz freshly grated Parmesan cheese, plus extra to serve (optional)

salt and pepper

fresh sage sprigs, to garnish

1 Warm a large serving dish or bowl. Bring a large pan of lightly salted water to the boil. Add the spaghetti and 1 tablespoon of the oil and cook until tender, but still firm to the bite. Drain, return to the pan and keep warm.

2 Meanwhile, heat the remaining oil in a frying pan over a medium heat. Add the onion and fry until it is transparent. Add the garlic and bacon and fry until the bacon is crisp. Transfer to the warm plate and keep warm.

3 Melt the butter in the frying pan. Add the sliced mushrooms and fry, stirring occasionally, for 3–4 minutes. Return the bacon and garlic mixture to the pan. Cover and keep warm.

4 Mix together the cream, eggs and cheese in a large bowl and season to taste with salt and pepper.

5 Working quickly, tip the spaghetti into the bacon mixture and pour over the egg mixture. Toss the spaghetti quickly into the mixture using 2 forks. Garnish with sage and extra Parmesan if you wish. Serve immediately.

### COOK'S TIP
The key to success with this recipe is not to overcook the egg. It is important to keep the ingredients hot enough just to cook the egg, and to work rapidly to avoid scrambling it.

# Spicy Chorizo Vermicelli

Simple and quick to make, this spicy dish will set the taste buds tingling, with its wild mushrooms, chillies and anchovies.

## NUTRITIONAL INFORMATION

| | | | |
|---|---|---|---|
| Calories | 672 | Sugars | 1g |
| Protein | 16g | Fat | 27g |
| Carbohydrate | 90g | Saturates | 6g |

 5 mins   10–12 mins

### SERVES 6

## I N G R E D I E N T S

680 g/1½ lb dried vermicelli

125 ml/4 fl oz olive oil

2 garlic cloves

125 g/4½ oz chorizo, sliced

225 g/8 oz wild mushrooms

3 fresh red chillies, chopped

2 tbsp freshly grated Parmesan cheese

salt and pepper

anchovy fillets, to garnish

1 Bring a large saucepan of lightly salted water to the boil. Add the vermicelli and 1 tablespoon of the oil and cook until just tender, but still firm to the bite. Drain, place on a large, warm, serving plate and keep warm.

2 Meanwhile heat the remaining oil in a large frying pan. Add the garlic and fry for 1 minute. Add the chorizo and wild mushrooms and cook for 4 minutes, then add the chopped chillies and cook for 1 further minute.

3 Pour the chorizo and wild mushroom mixture over the vermicelli and season with a little salt and pepper to taste. Sprinkle over freshly grated Parmesan cheese, garnish with a lattice of anchovy fillets and serve immediately.

## VARIATION

Fresh sardines may be used in this recipe in place of the anchovies. However, ensure that you gut and clean the sardines, removing the backbone, before using them.

# Tricolour Timballini

An unusual way of serving pasta, these cheese moulds are excellent with a crunchy salad for a light lunch.

## NUTRITIONAL INFORMATION

| | | | |
|---|---|---|---|
| Calories | ......529 | Sugars | ........7g |
| Protein | .......18g | Fat | ..........29g |
| Carbohydrate | ..46g | Saturates | .....12g |

 30 mins    1 hr

### SERVES 4

### INGREDIENTS

1 tbsp butter, softened

60 g/2 oz dried white breadcrumbs

175 g/6 oz dried tricolour spaghetti, broken into 5 cm/2 inch lengths

1 tbsp olive oil

1 egg yolk

125 g/4½ oz grated Gruyère cheese

300 ml/10 fl oz Béchamel Sauce (see page 38)

### TOMATO SAUCE

2 tbsp olive oil

1 onion, finely chopped

1 bay leaf

150 ml/5 fl oz dry white wine

150 ml/5 fl oz passata

1 tbsp tomato purée

salt and pepper

fresh basil leaves, to garnish

1 Butter four 180 ml/6 fl oz moulds or ramekins. Coat the insides with half of the breadcrumbs.

2 Bring a pan of lightly salted water to the boil. Add the spaghetti and olive oil and cook for 8–10 minutes or until just tender. Drain and transfer to a mixing bowl. Add the egg yolk and cheese to the pasta and season.

3 Pour the Béchamel Sauce into the bowl containing the pasta and mix. Spoon the mixture into the ramekins and sprinkle over the remaining breadcrumbs.

4 Stand the ramekins on a baking tray and bake in a preheated oven, 220°C/425°F/Gas Mark 7, for 20 minutes. Set aside for 10 minutes.

5 Meanwhile, make the sauce. Heat the olive oil in a pan and gently fry the chopped onion with the bay leaf for 2–3 minutes, stirring constantly.

6 Stir in the wine, passata and tomato purée and season with salt and pepper to taste. Simmer for 20 minutes, until thickened. Remove and discard the bay leaf. Turn the timballini out onto serving plates, garnish with the basil leaves and serve with the tomato sauce.

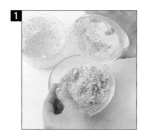

# Pasta with Bacon & Tomatoes

As this dish cooks, the mouth-watering aroma of bacon, sweet tomatoes and oregano is a feast in itself.

## NUTRITIONAL INFORMATION

| | | | |
|---|---|---|---|
| Calories | . . . . . . 431 | Sugars | . . . . . . . . 8g |
| Protein | . . . . . . . 10g | Fat | . . . . . . . . . . 9g |
| Carbohydrate | . . 34g | Saturates | . . . . . 14g |

 10 mins     35 mins

### SERVES 4

## I N G R E D I E N T S

900 g/2 lb small, sweet tomatoes

6 slices rindless smoked bacon

4 tbsp butter

1 onion, chopped

1 garlic clove, crushed

4 fresh oregano sprigs, finely chopped

450 g/1 lb dried orecchiette

1 tbsp olive oil

salt and pepper

freshly grated Pecorino cheese, to serve

1 Blanch the tomatoes in boiling water. Drain, skin and seed the tomatoes, then roughly chop the flesh.

2 Using a sharp knife, chop the bacon into evenly sized small dice.

3 Melt the butter in a saucepan. Add the bacon and fry until it is golden.

4 Add the onion and garlic and fry over a medium heat for 5–7 minutes, until just softened.

5 Add the tomatoes and oregano to the pan and then season to taste with salt and pepper. Lower the heat and simmer gently for 10–12 minutes.

6 Bring a large pan of lightly salted water to the boil. Add the orecchiette and oil and cook for 12 minutes, until just tender, but still firm to the bite. Drain the cooked pasta and transfer to a warm serving dish or bowl.

7 Spoon the bacon and tomato sauce over the pasta, toss to coat and serve with the cheese.

## COOK'S TIP

For an authentic Italian flavour use pancetta, rather than ordinary bacon. Pancetta is streaked with fat and adds rich undertones of flavour to many traditional dishes. It is available smoked or unsmoked from supermarkets and delicatessens.

# Spaghetti with Ricotta Cheese

This nutty pasta dish has a delicate flavour which is ideally suited to a light summer lunch.

## NUTRITIONAL INFORMATION

Calories . . . . . . . 714    Sugars . . . . . . . . 6g
Protein . . . . . . . 22g    Fat . . . . . . . . . . 41g
Carbohydrate . . 69g    Saturates . . . . . 14g

 5 mins     5–10 mins

### SERVES 4

## INGREDIENTS

350 g/12 oz dried spaghetti

3 tbsp olive oil

3 tbsp butter

2 tbsp chopped fresh flat leaf parsley

125 g/4½ oz freshly ground almonds

125 g/4½ oz ricotta cheese

pinch of grated nutmeg

pinch of ground cinnamon

150 ml/5 fl oz crème fraîche

125 ml/4 fl oz hot chicken stock

1 tbsp pine kernels

salt and pepper

fresh flat leaf parsley sprigs, to garnish

1 Bring a large pan of lightly salted water to the boil. Add the spaghetti and 1 tablespoon of the oil and cook until tender, but still firm to the bite.

2 Drain the pasta, return to the pan and toss with the butter and chopped parsley. Set aside and keep warm.

3 To make the sauce, mix together the ground almonds, ricotta cheese, nutmeg, cinnamon and crème fraîche over a low heat until it forms a thick paste. Gradually stir in the remaining oil. When the oil has been fully incorporated into the mixture, gradually stir in the hot chicken stock, until smooth. Season to taste with black pepper.

4 Transfer the spaghetti to a warm serving dish, pour over the sauce and toss together well (see Cook's Tip, right). Sprinkle over the pine kernels, garnish with the flat leaf parsley and serve warm.

### COOK'S TIP

Use two large forks to toss spaghetti, so that it is thoroughly coated with the sauce. Ease the prongs under the pasta on each side and lift them towards the centre. Continue this evenly and rhythmically until the pasta is completely coated.

# Smoked Salmon Spaghetti

Made in moments, this is a luxurious dish which can be used to astonish and delight any unexpected guests.

## NUTRITIONAL INFORMATION

| | |
|---|---|
| Calories ...... 949 | Sugars ........ 6g |
| Protein ....... 26g | Fat .......... 49g |
| Carbohydrate .. 86g | Saturates ..... 27g |

 5–10 mins    5 mins

### SERVES 4

## I N G R E D I E N T S

450 g/1 lb dried buckwheat spaghetti

2 tbsp olive oil

300 ml/10 fl oz double cream

150 ml/5 fl oz whisky or brandy

125 g/4½ oz smoked salmon

pinch of cayenne pepper

black pepper

2 tbsp chopped fresh coriander
   or parsley

90 g/3 oz feta cheese, well drained
   and crumbled

fresh coriander or parsley leaves,
   to garnish

1 Bring a large pan of lightly salted water to the boil. Add the spaghetti and 1 tablespoon of the olive oil and cook until tender, but still firm to the bite. Drain the spaghetti, return to the pan and sprinkle over the remaining olive oil. Cover, shake the pan, set aside and keep warm.

2 Pour the cream into a small saucepan and bring to simmering point, but do not let it boil. Pour the whisky or brandy into another small saucepan and bring to simmering point, but do not allow it to boil. Remove both pans from the heat and mix together the cream and whisky or brandy.

3 Cut the smoked salmon into thin strips and add to the cream mixture. Season to taste with cayenne and black pepper. Just before serving, stir in the chopped fresh coriander or parsley.

4 Transfer the spaghetti to a warm serving dish, pour over the sauce and toss thoroughly with 2 large forks. Scatter over the crumbled feta cheese, garnish with the coriander or parsley leaves and serve immediately.

## COOK'S TIP

Serve this rich and luxurious dish with a green salad tossed in a lemon-flavoured dressing.

# Spaghetti Olio e Aglio

This easy and satisfying Roman dish originated as a cheap meal for poor people, but has now become a favourite in restaurants and trattorias.

## NUTRITIONAL INFORMATION

| | | | |
|---|---|---|---|
| Calories | . . . . . . 515 | Sugars | . . . . . . . . 1g |
| Protein | . . . . . . . . 8g | Fat | . . . . . . . . . . 33g |
| Carbohydrate | . . 50g | Saturates | . . . . . . 5g |

 5 mins     5 mins

### SERVES 4

## I N G R E D I E N T S

125 ml/4 fl oz olive oil

3 garlic cloves, crushed

450 g/1 lb fresh spaghetti

3 tbsp roughly chopped fresh parsley

salt and pepper

1 Reserve 1 tablespoon of the olive oil and heat the remainder in a medium saucepan. Add the garlic and a pinch of salt and cook over a low heat, stirring constantly, until golden brown, then remove the pan from the heat. Do not allow the garlic to burn as it will taint the flavour. (If it does burn, you will have to start all over again.)

2 Meanwhile, bring a large saucepan of lightly salted water to the boil. Add the spaghetti and reserved olive oil to the pan and cook for 2–3 minutes, or until tender, but still firm to the bite. Drain the spaghetti thoroughly and return to the pan.

3 Add the oil and garlic mixture to the spaghetti and toss to coat thoroughly. Season with pepper, add the chopped fresh parsley and toss to coat again.

4 Transfer the spaghetti to a warm serving dish and serve immediately.

# Braised Fennel & Linguine

The aniseed flavour of the fennel gives that little extra punch to this delicious, creamy, pasta dish.

## NUTRITIONAL INFORMATION

| Calories | ...... 650 | Sugars | ........ 6g |
|----------|------------|--------|-------------|
| Protein | ....... 14g | Fat | .......... 39g |
| Carbohydrate | .. 62g | Saturates | ..... 22g |

20 mins     50 mins

### SERVES 4

## INGREDIENTS

6 fennel bulbs

150 ml/5 fl oz vegetable stock

2 tbsp butter

6 rashers rindless smoked bacon, diced

6 shallots, quartered

3 tbsp plain flour

100 ml/3½ fl oz double cream

1 tbsp Madeira

450 g/1 lb dried linguine

1 tbsp olive oil

salt and pepper

1 Trim the fennel bulbs, then peel off and reserve the outer layer of each. Cut the bulbs into quarters and put them in a large saucepan with the stock and the reserved outer layers.

2 Bring to the boil, lower the heat and simmer for 5 minutes.

3 Using a perforated spoon, transfer the fennel to a large dish. Discard the outer layers of the fennel bulbs. Bring the vegetable stock to the boil and allow to reduce by half. Set aside.

4 Melt the butter in a frying pan. Add the bacon and shallots and fry over a medium heat, stirring frequently, for 4 minutes. Add the flour, reduced stock, cream and Madeira and cook, stirring constantly, for 3 minutes or until the sauce is smooth. Season to taste with salt and pepper and pour over the fennel.

5 Bring a large saucepan of lightly salted water to the boil. Add the linguine and olive oil, bring back to the boil and cook for 8–10 minutes until tender but still firm to the bite. Drain and transfer to a deep ovenproof dish.

6 Add the fennel and sauce and braise in a preheated oven, 180°C/350°F/Gas Mark 4, for 20 minutes. Serve immediately.

## COOK'S TIP

Fennel will keep in the salad drawer of the refrigerator for 2–3 days, but it is best eaten as fresh as possible. Cut surfaces turn brown quickly, so do not prepare it too much in advance of cooking.

# Pasta Omelette

This is a superb way of using up any leftover pasta, such as penne, macaroni or conchiglie.

## NUTRITIONAL INFORMATION

| | | | |
|---|---|---|---|
| Calories | ...... 638 | Sugars | ........ 5g |
| Protein | ....... 24g | Fat | .......... 38g |
| Carbohydrate | .. 53g | Saturates | ...... 7g |

5 mins      15–20 mins

### SERVES 2

### I N G R E D I E N T S

4 tbsp olive oil

1 small onion, chopped

1 fennel bulb, thinly sliced

125 g/4½ oz potato, diced

1 garlic clove, chopped

4 eggs

1 tbsp chopped fresh flat leaf parsley

pinch of chilli powder

100 g/3½ oz cooked short pasta

2 tbsp stuffed green olives, halved

salt and pepper

fresh marjoram sprigs, to garnish

tomato salad, to serve

4 Heat 1 tablespoon of the remaining oil in a clean frying pan. Add half of the egg mixture to the pan, then add the cooked vegetables, pasta and half of the olives. Pour in the remaining egg mixture and cook until the sides begin to set.

5 Lift up the edges of the omelette with a palette knife to allow the uncooked egg to spread underneath. Cook, shaking the pan occasionally, until the underside is a light golden brown colour.

6 Slide the omelette out of the pan onto a plate. Wipe the pan with kitchen paper and heat the remaining oil. Invert the omelette into the pan and cook until the other side is golden brown.

7 Slide the omelette onto a warmed serving dish and garnish with the remaining olives and the marjoram. Serve cut into wedges, with a tomato salad.

1 Heat half the oil in a heavy-based frying pan over a low heat. Add the onion, fennel and potato and fry, stirring occasionally, for 8–10 minutes, until the potato is just tender.

2 Stir in the chopped garlic and cook for 1 minute. Remove the pan from the heat, transfer the vegetables to a plate and set aside to keep warm.

3 Beat the eggs until they are frothy. Stir in the parsley and season with salt, pepper and a pinch of chilli powder.

# Fettuccine all'Alfredo

This simple, traditional dish can be made with any long pasta, but is especially good with flat noodles, such as fettuccine or tagliatelle.

## NUTRITIONAL INFORMATION

| | | | |
|---|---|---|---|
| Calories | . . . . . . 540 | Sugars | . . . . . . . . 2g |
| Protein | . . . . . . . 15g | Fat | . . . . . . . . . . 40g |
| Carbohydrate | . . 31g | Saturates | . . . . . 23g |

5 mins   5 mins

### SERVES 4

## INGREDIENTS

2 tbsp butter

200 ml/7 fl oz double cream

450 g/1 lb fresh fettuccine

1 tbsp olive oil

90 g/3 oz freshly grated Parmesan cheese, plus extra to serve

pinch of freshly grated nutmeg

salt and pepper

fresh flat leaf parsley sprig, to garnish

1 Put the butter and 150 ml/5 fl oz of the cream in a large saucepan and bring the mixture to the boil over a medium heat. Reduce the heat and then simmer gently for about 1 1/2 minutes, or until the cream has slightly thickened.

2 Meanwhile, bring a large pan of lightly salted water to the boil. Add the fettuccine and olive oil and cook for 2–3 minutes, until tender but still firm to the bite. Drain the fettuccine thoroughly and return it to the warm pan, then pour over the cream sauce.

3 Toss the fettuccine in the sauce over a low heat, stirring with a wooden spoon, until thoroughly coated.

4 Add the remaining cream, Parmesan cheese and nutmeg to the fettuccine mixture and season to taste with salt and pepper. Toss thoroughly to coat while gently heating through.

5 Transfer the fettucine mixture to a warm serving plate and garnish with the fresh flat leaf parsley sprig. Serve immediately, handing extra grated Parmesan cheese separately.

## VARIATION

This classic Roman dish is often served with the addition of strips of ham and fresh peas. Add 225 g/8 oz shelled cooked peas and 175 g/6 oz ham strips with the Parmesan cheese in step 4.

# Pistou

This hearty soup of beans and vegetables is from Nice and gets its name from the fresh basil sauce stirred in at the last minute.

## NUTRITIONAL INFORMATION

| | | | |
|---|---|---|---|
| Calories | 55 | Sugars | 1.2g |
| Protein | 3.8g | Fat | 2.6g |
| Carbohydrate | 4.2g | Saturates | 0.6g |

 10 mins   25 mins

### SERVES 6

## INGREDIENTS

2 young carrots

450 g/1 lb potatoes

200 g/7 oz fresh peas in their shells

200 g/7 oz thin green beans

150 g/5½ oz young courgettes

2 tbsp olive oil

1 garlic clove, crushed

1 large onion, finely chopped

2.5 litres/4½ pints vegetable stock or water

1 bouquet garni or 2 fresh parsley sprigs and 1 bay leaf tied in a 7.5 cm/3 inch piece of celery

85 g/3 oz dried small soup pasta

1 large tomato, skinned, deseeded and chopped or diced

pared Parmesan cheese, to serve

### PISTOU SAUCE

75 g/2¾ oz fresh basil leaves

1 garlic clove

5 tbsp fruity extra-virgin olive oil

salt and pepper

1 To make the pistou sauce, put the basil leaves, garlic and olive oil in a food processor and process until well blended. Season with salt and pepper to taste. Transfer to a bowl, cover with clingfilm and chill until required.

2 Peel the carrots and cut them in half lengthways, then slice. Peel the potatoes and cut into quarters lengthways, then slice. Set aside in a bowl of water until ready to use, to prevent discoloration.

3 Shell the peas. Top and tail the beans and cut them into 2.5cm/1inch pieces. Cut the courgettes in half lengthways, then cut across into slices.

4 Heat the oil in a large saucepan or flameproof casserole. Add the garlic and fry for 2 minutes, stirring. Add the onion and continue frying for 2 minutes until soft. Add the carrots and potatoes and stir for about 30 seconds.

5 Pour in the stock and bring to the boil. Lower the heat, partially cover and simmer for 8 minutes, until the vegetables are starting to become tender.

6 Stir in the peas, beans, courgettes, bouquet garni, pasta and tomato. Season and cook for 4 minutes, or until the vegetables and pasta are tender. Stir in the pistou sauce and serve with Parmesan.

# Spinach & Herb Orzo

Serve this vibrant green pasta dish with any grilled meat or seafood. Orzo, shaped like long grains of barley, is popular in southern Italy and Greece.

## NUTRITIONAL INFORMATION

| | | | |
|---|---|---|---|
| Calories | 304 | Sugars | 8g |
| Protein | 12g | Fat | 6g |
| Carbohydrate | 54g | Saturates | 1g |

15–20 mins     10 mins

### SERVES 4

## INGREDIENTS

1 tsp salt

250 g/9 oz dried orzo

200 g/7 oz baby spinach leaves

150 g/5½ oz rocket

25 g/1 oz fresh flat leaf parsley leaves

25 g/1 oz fresh coriander leaves

4 spring onions

2 tbsp extra-virgin olive oil

1 tbsp garlic-flavoured olive oil

pepper

### TO SERVE

radicchio or other lettuce leaves

60 g/2 oz feta cheese, well drained and crumbled (optional)

lemon slices

1 Bring 2 pans of water to the boil, and put 12 ice cubes in a bowl of cold water. Add the salt and orzo to one of the pans, return to the boil and cook for 8–10 minutes, or according to packet instructions, until the pasta is tender.

2 Meanwhile, remove any tough spinach stems. Rinse the leaves well to remove any grit. Chop the rocket, parsley, coriander and green parts of the spring onions.

3 Put the spinach, rocket, parsley, coriander and spring onions in the other pan of boiling water and blanch for 15 seconds. Drain and transfer to the iced water to preserve the colour.

4 When the spinach, herbs and spring onions are cool, squeeze out all the excess water. Transfer to a small food processor and process. Add the olive oil and garlic-flavoured oil and process again until the mixture is well blended.

5 Drain the orzo well and stir in the spinach mixture. Toss well and adjust the seasoning.

6 Line a serving platter with radicchio leaves and pile the orzo on top. Sprinkle with feta cheese, if desired, and garnish with lemon slices. Serve hot or leave to cool to room temperature.

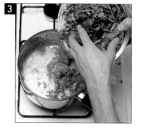

# Brown Lentil & Pasta Soup

In Italy, this soup is called *Minestrade Lentiche*. A minestra is a soup cooked with pasta; here, farfalline, a small bow-shaped variety, is used.

## NUTRITIONAL INFORMATION

| | | | |
|---|---|---|---|
| Calories | 225 | Sugars | 1g |
| Protein | 13g | Fat | 8g |
| Carbohydrate | 27g | Saturates | 3g |

 5 mins     25 mins

### SERVES 4

### INGREDIENTS

4 rashers streaky bacon, cut into small squares

1 onion, chopped

2 garlic cloves, crushed

2 celery sticks, chopped

50 g/1¾ oz farfalline or spaghetti, broken into small pieces

400 g/14 oz canned brown lentils, drained

1.2 litres/2 pints hot ham or vegetable stock

2 tbsp chopped fresh mint

1 Place the bacon in a large frying pan together with the onion, garlic and celery. Dry fry for 4–5 minutes, stirring, until the onion is tender and the bacon is just beginning to brown.

2 Add the pasta to the pan and cook, stirring, for about 1 minute to coat the pasta thoroughly in the oil.

3 Add the brown lentils and the ham or vegetable stock and bring the mixture to the boil. Reduce the heat and leave to simmer for 12–15 minutes or until the pasta is tender.

4 Remove the pan from the heat and stir in the chopped fresh mint.

5 Transfer the soup to warm soup bowls and serve immediately.

## COOK'S TIP

If you prefer to use dried lentils, add the stock before the pasta and cook for 1–1¼ hours until the lentils are tender. Add the pasta and cook for a further 12–15 minutes.

# Italian Fish Stew

This robust stew is full of Mediterranean flavours. If you do not want to prepare the fish yourself, ask your local fishmonger to do it for you.

## NUTRITIONAL INFORMATION

| | | |
|---|---|---|
| Calories ......236 | Sugars ........4g | |
| Protein .......20g | Fat ...........7g | |
| Carbohydrate ..25g | Saturates ......1g | |

 5–10 mins      25 mins

### SERVES 4

## I N G R E D I E N T S

2 tbsp olive oil

2 red onions, finely chopped

1 garlic clove, crushed

2 courgettes, sliced

400 g/14 oz canned chopped tomatoes

850 ml/1½ pints fish or vegetable stock

90 g/3 oz dried pasta shapes

350 g/12 oz firm white fish, such as cod, haddock or hake

1 tbsp chopped fresh basil or oregano or 1 tsp dried oregano

1 tsp grated lemon rind

1 tbsp cornflour

1 tbsp water

salt and pepper

fresh basil or oregano sprigs, to garnish

3 Skin and bone the fish, then cut it into chunks. Add the fish chunks to the saucepan with the basil or oregano and lemon rind and cook gently for 5 minutes until the fish is opaque and flakes easily (take care not to overcook it).

4 Blend the cornflour with the water and stir into the stew. Cook gently for 2 minutes, stirring, until thickened. Season with salt and pepper to taste and ladle into warmed soup bowls. Garnish with basil or oregano sprigs and serve at once.

1 Heat the oil in a large saucepan and fry the onions and garlic for 5 minutes. Add the courgettes and cook for 2–3 minutes, stirring often.

2 Add the tomatoes and stock to the saucepan and bring to the boil. Add the pasta, cover the pan and reduce the heat. Simmer for 5 minutes.

# Spinach & Anchovy Pasta

This colourful light meal can be made with a variety of different pasta, including spaghetti and linguine.

## NUTRITIONAL INFORMATION

| | | |
|---|---|---|
| Calories . . . . . . 619 | Sugars . . . . . . . . 5g |
| Protein . . . . . . . 21g | Fat . . . . . . . . . . 31g |
| Carbohydrate . . 67g | Saturates . . . . . . 3g |

 10 mins      25 mins

### SERVES 4

## I N G R E D I E N T S

900 g/2 lb fresh, young spinach leaves

400 g/14 oz dried fettuccine

6 tbsp olive oil

3 tbsp pine kernels

3 garlic cloves, crushed

8 canned anchovy fillets, drained and chopped

salt

1 Trim off any tough spinach stalks. Rinse the spinach leaves and place them in a large saucepan with only the water that clings to them after washing. Cover and cook over a high heat, shaking the pan from time, until the spinach has wilted, but retains its bright green colour. Drain well, set aside and keep warm.

2 Bring a large saucepan of lightly salted water to the boil. Add the fettuccine and 1 tablespoon of the oil and cook for 8–10 minutes until it is just tender, but still firm to the bite.

3 Heat 4 tablespoons of the remaining oil in a saucepan. Add the pine kernels to the pan and fry until they turn golden. Remove the pine kernels from the pan and set aside until required.

4 Add the garlic to the pan and fry until golden. Add the anchovies and stir in the spinach. Cook, stirring, for 2–3 minutes, until heated through. Return the pine kernels to the pan.

5 Drain the fettuccine, toss in the remaining olive oil and transfer to a warm serving dish. Spoon the anchovy and spinach sauce over the fettuccine, toss lightly and serve immediately.

## COOK'S TIP

If you are in a hurry, you can use frozen leaf spinach. Defrost and drain thoroughly, pressing out as much moisture as possible. Cut the leaves into strips and add to the dish with the anchovies in step 4.

# Spaghetti Bolognese

You can use this classic meat sauce for lasagne, cannelloni or any other baked pasta dishes.

## NUTRITIONAL INFORMATION

| Calories ...... 732 | Sugars ....... 15g |
|---|---|
| Protein ....... 39g | Fat .......... 20g |
| Carbohydrate .. 96g | Saturates ...... 5g |

 5 mins        1¼ hrs

### SERVES 4

3 tbsp olive oil

2 garlic cloves, crushed

1 large onion, finely chopped

1 carrot, diced

225 g/8 oz lean minced beef, veal
  or chicken

85 g/3 oz chicken livers, finely chopped

100 g/3½ oz lean, Parma ham, diced

150 ml/5 fl oz Marsala

280 g/10 oz canned chopped
  plum tomatoes

1 tbsp chopped fresh basil leaves

2 tbsp tomato purée

salt and pepper

450 g/1 lb dried spaghetti

1 Heat 2 tablespoons of the olive oil in a large saucepan. Add the garlic, onion and carrot and fry for 6 minutes.

2 Add the minced beef, veal or chicken, chicken livers and Parma ham to the pan and cook over a medium heat for 12 minutes, until well browned.

3 Stir the Marsala, tomatoes, basil and tomato purée into the pan and cook for 4 minutes. Season the sauce to taste with salt and pepper. Cover and simmer for about 30 minutes.

4 Remove the lid from the pan, stir and simmer for a further 15 minutes.

5 Meanwhile, bring a large pan of lightly salted water to the boil. Add the spaghetti and the remaining oil and cook for about 12 minutes, or until tender, but still firm to the bite. Drain and transfer to a serving dish. Pour the sauce over the pasta, toss and serve hot.

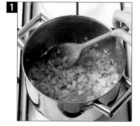  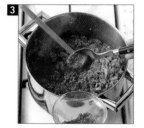

## VARIATION

Chicken livers are an essential ingredient in a classic Bolognese sauce, to which they add richness. However, if you prefer not to use them, you can substitute the same quantity of minced beef.

# Creamed Strips of Sirloin

This quick and easy dish tastes superb and would make a delicious treat for a special occasion.

## NUTRITIONAL INFORMATION

Calories ...... 796  Sugars ........ 2g
Protein ....... 29g  Fat .......... 63g
Carbohydrate .. 26g  Saturates ..... 39g

15 mins       30 mins

### SERVES 4

## I N G R E D I E N T S

6 tbsp butter

450 g/1 lb sirloin steak, trimmed and cut into thin strips

175 g/6 oz button mushrooms, sliced

1 tsp mustard

pinch of freshly grated root ginger

2 tbsp dry sherry

150 ml/5 fl oz double cream

salt and pepper

4 slices hot toast, cut into triangles, to serve

### P A S T A

450 g/1 lb dried rigatoni

2 tbsp olive oil

2 fresh basil sprigs

115 g/4 oz butter

1 Melt the butter in a large frying pan and gently fry the steak over a low heat, stirring frequently, for 6 minutes. Using a slotted spoon, transfer the steak to an ovenproof dish and keep warm.

2 Add the sliced mushrooms to the frying pan and cook for 2–3 minutes in the juices remaining in the pan. Add the mustard, ginger, salt and pepper. Cook for 2 minutes, then add the sherry and cream. Cook for a further 3 minutes, then pour the cream sauce over the steak.

3 Bake the steak and cream mixture in a preheated oven, 190°C/375°F/Gas Mark 5, for 10 minutes.

4 Meanwhile, bring a large saucepan of lightly salted water to the boil. Add the rigatoni, olive oil and 1 of the basil sprigs and boil rapidly for 10 minutes, or until tender but firm to the bite. Drain and transfer to a warm serving plate. Toss the pasta with the butter and garnish with the other sprig of basil.

5 Serve the creamed steak strips with the pasta and triangles of hot toast.

## COOK'S TIP

Dried pasta will keep for up to 6 months. Keep it in the packet and reseal it once you have opened it, or transfer it to an airtight jar.

# Fresh Spaghetti & Meatballs

This well-loved Italian dish is famous across the world. Make the most of it by using high-quality steak for the meatballs.

## NUTRITIONAL INFORMATION

Calories ...... 665    Sugars ........ 9g
Protein ....... 39g    Fat .......... 24g
Carbohydrate .. 77g    Saturates ...... 8g

 45 mins     1¼ hrs

### SERVES 4

## INGREDIENTS

150 g/5½ oz brown breadcrumbs

150 ml/5 fl oz milk

2 tbsp butter

3 tbsp wholemeal flour

200 ml/7 fl oz beef stock

400 g/14 oz canned chopped tomatoes

2 tbsp tomato purée

1 tsp sugar

1 tbsp finely chopped fresh tarragon

1 large onion, chopped

450 g/1 lb minced steak

1 tsp paprika

4 tbsp olive oil

450 g/1 lb fresh spaghetti

salt and pepper

fresh tarragon sprigs, to garnish

1 Place the brown breadcrumbs in a bowl, add the milk and set aside to soak for about 30 minutes.

2 Melt half of the butter in a pan. Add the flour and cook, stirring constantly, for 2 minutes. Gradually stir in the beef stock and cook, stirring constantly, for a further 5 minutes. Add the tomatoes, tomato purée, sugar and tarragon. Season well and simmer for 25 minutes.

3 Mix the onion, steak and paprika into the breadcrumbs. Season to taste. Shape the mixture into 14 meatballs.

4 Heat the oil and remaining butter in a frying pan and fry the meatballs, turning, until brown all over. Place the meatballs in a deep casserole, pour over the tomato sauce, cover and bake in a preheated oven, 180°C/350°F/Gas Mark 4, for 25 minutes.

5 Bring a large saucepan of lightly salted water to the boil. Add the spaghetti, bring back to the boil and cook for about 2–3 minutes, or until tender, but firm to the bite.

6 Remove the meatballs from the oven and allow them to cool for 3 minutes. Serve the meatballs and their sauce with the spaghetti, garnished with fresh tarragon sprigs.

# Pasticcio

A recipe that has both Italian and Greek origins, this dish may be served hot or cold, cut into thick, satisfying squares.

## NUTRITIONAL INFORMATION

| | | |
|---|---|---|
| Calories ...... 590 | Sugars ........ 8g | |
| Protein ....... 34g | Fat .......... 39g | |
| Carbohydrate .. 23g | Saturates ..... 16g | |

35 mins    1¼ hrs

### SERVES 6

## INGREDIENTS

225 g/8 oz fusilli, or other short pasta shapes

1 tbsp olive oil

4 tbsp double cream

rosemary sprigs, to garnish

### SAUCE

2 tbsp olive oil, plus extra for brushing

1 onion, thinly sliced

1 red pepper, deseeded and chopped

2 garlic cloves, chopped

625 g/1 lb 6 oz lean minced beef

400 g/14 oz canned chopped tomatoes

125 ml/4 fl oz dry white wine

2 tbsp chopped fresh parsley

50 g/1¾ oz canned anchovies, drained and chopped

salt and pepper

### TOPPING

300 ml/10 fl oz natural yogurt

3 eggs

pinch of freshly grated nutmeg

40 g/1½ oz freshly grated Parmesan cheese

1 To make the sauce, heat the oil in a large frying pan and fry the onion and red pepper for 3 minutes. Stir in the garlic and cook for 1 minute more. Stir in the beef and cook, stirring frequently, until it is no longer pink.

2 Add the tomatoes and wine to the pan, stir well and bring to the boil. Simmer, uncovered, for 20 minutes or until the sauce is fairly thick. Stir in the parsley and anchovies and season to taste.

3 Cook the pasta in a large pan of boiling salted water, adding the oil, for 8–10 minutes or until tender. Drain and transfer to a bowl. Stir in the cream and set aside.

4 To make the topping, beat together the yogurt, eggs and nutmeg until they are well combined, and season with salt and pepper to taste.

5 Brush a large, shallow ovenproof dish with oil. Spoon in half of the pasta mixture and cover with half of the meat sauce. Repeat these layers, then spread the topping evenly over the final layer. Sprinkle the grated Parmesan cheese evenly on top.

6 Bake in a preheated oven, 190°C/ 375°F/Gas Mark 5, for 25 minutes or until the topping is golden brown and bubbling. Garnish with sprigs of fresh rosemary and serve immediately.

# Neapolitan Veal Cutlets

The delicious combination of apple, onion and mushroom perfectly complements the delicate flavour of veal.

## NUTRITIONAL INFORMATION

Calories . . . . . . 1071    Sugars . . . . . . . 13g
Protein . . . . . . . 74g    Fat . . . . . . . . . . 59g
Carbohydrate . . 66g    Saturates . . . . . 16g

 20 mins     45 mins

### SERVES 4

## INGREDIENTS

200 g/7 oz butter

4 x 250 g/9 oz veal cutlets, trimmed

1 large onion, sliced

2 apples, peeled, cored and sliced

175 g/6 oz button mushrooms

1 tbsp chopped fresh tarragon

8 black peppercorns

1 tbsp sesame seeds

400 g/14 oz dried marille

100 ml/3½ fl oz extra virgin olive oil

2 large beef tomatoes, cut in half

175 g/6 oz mascarpone cheese

leaves of 1 fresh basil sprig

salt and pepper

fresh basil leaves, to garnish

3 Melt the remaining butter in the frying pan, then gently fry the button mushrooms, tarragon and peppercorns over a low heat for 3 minutes. Sprinkle over the sesame seeds.

4 Bring a pan of salted water to the boil. Add the pasta and 1 tablespoon of oil. Cook for 8–10 minutes, or until tender, but firm to the bite. Drain. Transfer to a plate.

5 Grill or fry the halved tomatoes with the basil for 2–3 minutes.

6 Top the pasta with the mascarpone cheese and sprinkle over the remaining olive oil. Place the onions, apples and veal cutlets on top of the pasta. Spoon the mushrooms, peppercorns and pan juices onto the cutlets, arrange the tomatoes and basil leaves around the edge and place in a preheated oven, 150°C/300°F/Gas Mark 2, for 5 minutes.

7 Season to taste with salt and pepper, garnish with fresh basil leaves and serve immediately.

1 Melt 4 tablespoons of the butter in a frying pan. Fry the veal over a low heat for 5 minutes on each side. Transfer to a dish and keep warm.

2 Fry the onion and apples in the pan until lightly browned. Transfer to a dish, place the veal on top and keep warm.

# Tagliatelle with Pumpkin

This unusual dish comes from the Emilia Romagna region. Why not serve it with Lambrusco, the local wine?

## NUTRITIONAL INFORMATION

Calories . . . . . . 559   Sugars . . . . . . . . 7g
Protein . . . . . . . 17g   Fat . . . . . . . . . . 32g
Carbohydrate . . 55g   Saturates . . . . . 14g

5 mins          20–25 mins

### SERVES 4

## I N G R E D I E N T S

500 g/1 lb 2 oz pumpkin or butternut
   squash, peeled and deseeded

3 tbsp olive oil

1 onion, finely chopped

2 garlic cloves, crushed

4–6 tbsp chopped fresh parsley

pinch of freshly grated nutmeg

about 250 ml/9 fl oz chicken or
   vegetable stock

115 g/4 oz Parma ham, cut into small pieces

250 g/9 oz dried tagliatelle

150 ml/5 fl oz double cream

salt and pepper

freshly grated Parmesan cheese, to serve

3 Add the pumpkin or squash pieces and cook for 2–3 minutes. Season to taste with salt, pepper and nutmeg.

4 Add half the stock to the pan, bring to the boil, cover and simmer for about 10 minutes, or until the pumpkin or squash is tender. Add more stock if the pumpkin or squash is becoming dry and looks as if it might be about to burn.

5 Add the pieces of Parma ham to the pan and cook, stirring frequently, for a further 2 minutes.

6 Meanwhile, bring a large saucepan of lightly salted water to the boil. Add the tagliatelle and the remaining 1 tablespoon of olive oil and cook for 12 minutes, until the pasta is tender but still firm to the bite. Drain the pasta and transfer to a warm serving dish.

7 Stir the cream into the pumpkin and ham mixture and heat well through. Spoon the mixture over the tagliatelle, sprinkle over the remaining chopped parsley to garnish, and serve hot. Hand round the grated Parmesan separately.

1 Cut the pumpkin or butternut squash in half and scoop out the seeds with a spoon. Cut the pumpkin or squash into 1 cm/½ inch dice.

2 Heat 2 tablespoons of the olive oil in a large saucepan. Add the onion and garlic and fry over a low heat for about 3 minutes, until soft. Add half the parsley and fry for 1 minute.

# Chicken Suprême Spaghetti

The refreshing combination of chicken and orange sauce makes this a perfect dish for a warm summer evening.

## NUTRITIONAL INFORMATION

Calories ...... 933  Sugars ....... 34g
Protein ....... 74g  Fat .......... 24g
Carbohydrate . 100g  Saturates ...... 5g

 5 mins    20 mins

### SERVES 4

## INGREDIENTS

2 tbsp rapeseed oil

3 tbsp olive oil

4 x 225 g/8 oz chicken suprêmes

150 ml/5 fl oz orange brandy

2 tbsp plain flour

150 ml/5 fl oz freshly squeezed orange juice

25 g/1 oz courgette, cut into matchsticks

25 g/1 oz leek, finely shredded

25 g/1 oz red pepper, cut into matchsticks

400 g/14 oz dried wholemeal spaghetti

3 large oranges, peeled and cut into segments

rind of 1 orange, cut into very fine strips

2 tbsp chopped fresh tarragon

150 ml/5 fl oz fromage frais or ricotta cheese

salt and pepper

fresh tarragon leaves, to garnish

1 Heat the rapeseed oil and 1 tablespoon of the olive oil in a frying pan. Add the chicken and cook quickly until golden brown. Add the orange brandy and cook for 3 minutes. Sprinkle over the flour and cook for 2 minutes.

2 Lower the heat and add the orange juice, courgette, leek and pepper and season. Simmer for 5 minutes until the sauce has thickened.

3 Meanwhile, bring a pan of salted water to the boil. Add the spaghetti and 1 tablespoon of the olive oil and cook for 10 minutes. Drain, transfer to a serving dish and drizzle over the remaining oil.

4 Add half the orange segments, half the orange rind, the tarragon and fromage frais or ricotta cheese to the sauce in the pan and cook for 3 minutes.

5 Place the chicken on top of the pasta, pour over a little sauce, garnish with the remaining orange segments and rind and tarragon, and serve immediately.

# Pasta with Chicken Sauce

Spinach ribbon noodles, topped with a rich tomato sauce and creamy chicken, make a very appetising dish.

## NUTRITIONAL INFORMATION

| | | | |
|---|---|---|---|
| Calories | 995 | Sugars | 8g |
| Protein | 36g | Fat | 74g |
| Carbohydrate | 50g | Saturates | 34g |

 15 mins     45 mins

### SERVES 4

## INGREDIENTS

250 g/9 oz fresh green tagliatelle

1 tbsp olive oil

fresh basil leaves, to garnish

### TOMATO SAUCE

2 tbsp olive oil

1 small onion, chopped

1 garlic clove, chopped

400 g/14 oz canned chopped tomatoes

2 tbsp chopped fresh parsley

1 tsp dried oregano

2 bay leaves

2 tbsp tomato purée

1 tsp sugar

salt and pepper

### CHICKEN SAUCE

4 tbsp unsalted butter

400 g/14 oz boned chicken breasts, skinned and cut into thin strips

90 g/3 oz blanched almonds

300 ml/10 fl oz double cream

salt and pepper

1 To make the tomato sauce, heat the oil in a pan over a medium heat. Add the onion and fry until translucent. Add the garlic and fry for 1 minute. Stir in the tomatoes, parsley, oregano, bay leaves, tomato purée, sugar and salt and pepper to taste, bring to the boil and simmer, uncovered, for 15–20 minutes, until reduced by half. Remove the pan from the heat and discard the bay leaves.

2 To make the chicken sauce, gently melt the butter in a frying pan over a medium heat. Add the chicken and almonds and stir-fry for 5–6 minutes, or until the chicken is cooked through.

3 Meanwhile, bring the cream to the boil in a small pan over a low heat and boil for about 10 minutes, until reduced by almost half. Pour the cream over the chicken and almonds, stir and season to taste with salt and pepper. Set aside and keep warm.

4 Bring a large pan of lightly salted water to the boil. Add the tagliatelle and olive oil and cook for 8–10 minutes until tender, but still firm to the bite. Drain and transfer to a warm serving dish. Spoon over the tomato sauce and arrange the chicken sauce down the centre. Garnish with the basil leaves and serve immediately.

# Mustard Baked Chicken

Chicken pieces are cooked in a succulent, mild mustard sauce, then coated in poppy seeds and served on a bed of fresh pasta shells.

## NUTRITIONAL INFORMATION

Calories ...... 652   Sugars ........ 5g
Protein ....... 51g   Fat .......... 31g
Carbohydrate .. 46g   Saturates ..... 12g

 10 mins    35 mins

### SERVES 4

## I N G R E D I E N T S

8 x 115 g/4 oz chicken pieces

4 tbsp butter, melted

4 tbsp mild mustard (see Cook's Tip)

2 tbsp lemon juice

1 tbsp brown sugar

1 tsp paprika

3 tbsp poppy seeds

400 g/14 oz fresh pasta shells

1 tbsp olive oil

salt and pepper

1 Arrange the chicken pieces in a single layer in a large ovenproof dish.

2 Mix together the butter, mustard, lemon juice, sugar and paprika in a bowl and season with salt and pepper to taste. Brush half of the mixture over the

upper surfaces of the chicken pieces and bake in a preheated oven, 200°C/400°F/Gas Mark 6, for 15 minutes.

3 Remove the dish from the oven and carefully turn over the chicken pieces. Coat the upper surfaces of the chicken with the remaining mustard mixture, sprinkle the chicken pieces with poppy seeds and return to the oven for a further 15 minutes.

4 Meanwhile, bring a large saucepan of lightly salted water to the boil for the pasta shells. Add the pasta and olive oil and cook for 8–10 minutes, or until tender, but still firm to the bite.

5 Drain the pasta thoroughly and arrange on a warmed serving dish. Top the pasta with the chicken, pour over the sauce and serve immediately.

## COOK'S TIP

Dijon is the type of mustard most often used in cooking, as it has a clean and only mildly spicy flavour. German mustard has a sweet-sour taste, and Bavarian mustard is slightly sweeter. American mustard is mild and sweet.

# Chicken & Lobster on Penne

While this is certainly a treat to get the taste buds tingling, it is not as extravagant as it sounds.

## NUTRITIONAL INFORMATION

| | | | |
|---|---|---|---|
| Calories | 696 | Sugars | 4g |
| Protein | 59g | Fat | 32g |
| Carbohydrate | 45g | Saturates | 9g |

 20 mins  30 mins

### SERVES 6

## INGREDIENTS

butter, for greasing

6 chicken suprêmes

450 g/1 lb dried penne rigate

6 tbsp extra virgin olive oil

90 g/3 oz freshly grated Parmesan cheese

### FILLING

115 g/4 oz lobster meat, chopped

2 shallots, very finely chopped

2 figs, chopped

1 tbsp Marsala

2 tbsp breadcrumbs

1 large egg, beaten

salt and pepper

1  Grease 6 pieces of foil large enough to enclose each chicken suprême and lightly grease a baking tray.

2  Place all of the filling ingredients into a mixing bowl and blend together thoroughly with a spoon.

3  Cut a pocket in each chicken suprême with a sharp knife and fill with the lobster mixture. Wrap each chicken suprême in foil, place the parcels on the greased baking tray and bake in a preheated oven, 200°C/ 400°F/Gas Mark 6, for 30 minutes.

4  Meanwhile, bring a large pan of lightly salted water to the boil. Add the pasta and 1 tablespoon of the olive oil and cook for about 10 minutes, or until tender but still firm to the bite. Drain the pasta thoroughly and transfer to a large serving plate. Sprinkle over the remaining olive oil and the grated Parmesan cheese, set aside and keep warm.

5  Carefully remove the foil from around the chicken suprêmes. Slice the suprêmes very thinly, arrange the slices over the pasta and serve immediately.

## COOK'S TIP

The cut of chicken known as suprême consists of the breast and wing. It is always skinned.

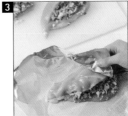

# Slices of Duckling with Pasta

A raspberry and honey sauce superbly counterbalances the richness of tender slices of duckling.

## NUTRITIONAL INFORMATION

| | | | |
|---|---|---|---|
| Calories | ...... 686 | Sugars | ....... 15g |
| Protein | ....... 62g | Fat | .......... 20g |
| Carbohydrate | .. 70g | Saturates | ...... 7g |

 15 mins   25 mins

### SERVES 4

## I N G R E D I E N T S

4 x 275 g/9 oz boned breasts of duckling

2 tbsp butter

50 g/1¾ oz finely chopped carrots

50 g/1¾ oz finely chopped shallots

1 tbsp lemon juice

150 ml/5 fl oz meat stock

4 tbsp clear honey

115 g/4 oz fresh or defrosted frozen raspberries

3 tbsp plain flour

1 tbsp Worcestershire sauce

400 g/14 oz fresh linguine

1 tbsp olive oil

salt and pepper

### TO GARNISH

fresh sprig of flat-leaved parsley

fresh raspberries

1 Trim and score the duck breasts with a sharp knife and season well all over. Melt the butter in a frying pan, add the duck breasts and fry until lightly coloured on both sides.

2 Add the carrots, shallots, lemon juice and half the meat stock and simmer over a low heat for 1 minute. Stir in half of the honey and half of the raspberries. Sprinkle over half of the flour and cook, stirring constantly, for 3 minutes. Season with pepper to taste and add the Worcestershire sauce.

3 Stir in the remaining meat stock and cook for 1 minute. Stir in the remaining honey and the rest of the raspberries and sprinkle over the remaining flour. Cook for a further 3 minutes.

4 Remove the duck and leave the sauce to simmer over a very low heat.

5 Meanwhile, bring a large saucepan of lightly salted water to the boil. Add the linguine and oil and cook for 8–10 minutes, or until tender, but firm to the bite. Drain and divide onto serving plates.

6 Slice the duck breast lengthways into 5 mm/¼ inch thick pieces. Pour a little sauce over the pasta and arrange the slices in a fan shape on top. Garnish with parsley and raspberries and serve immediately.

  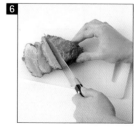

# Pasta-stuffed Tomatoes

This unusual and inexpensive dish would make a good starter for eight people or a delicious lunch for four.

## NUTRITIONAL INFORMATION

Calories .......298  Sugars .........4g
Protein ........10g  Fat ..........20g
Carbohydrate ...20g  Saturates .......5g

 15 mins    35 mins

### SERVES 4

## INGREDIENTS

5 tbsp extra virgin olive oil, plus extra for greasing

8 beef tomatoes or large round tomatoes

115 g/4 oz dried ditalini or other very small pasta shapes

8 black olives, stoned and finely chopped

2 tbsp finely chopped fresh basil

1 tbsp finely chopped fresh parsley

55 g/2 oz freshly grated Parmesan cheese

salt and pepper

fresh basil sprigs, to garnish

1 Prepare a baking tray by brushing with olive oil. Set aside.

2 Slice the tops off the tomatoes and reserve to make 'lids'. If the tomatoes will not stand up, cut a thin slice off the bottom of each tomato.

3 Using a teaspoon, scoop out the tomato pulp into a sieve, but do not pierce the tomato shells. Invert the tomato shells onto kitchen paper, pat dry and set aside to drain.

4 Bring a large saucepan of lightly salted water to the boil. Add the ditalini or other pasta and 1 tablespoon of the remaining olive oil and cook for 8-10 minutes or until tender, but still firm to the bite. Drain the pasta and set aside.

5 Put the olives, basil, parsley and Parmesan cheese into a large mixing bowl and stir in the drained tomato pulp. Add the pasta to the bowl. Stir in the remaining olive oil, mix together well and season to taste with salt and pepper.

6 Arrange the tomatoes on the baking tray. Spoon the pasta mixture into the tomato shells and replace the lids. Bake in a preheated oven,190°C/ 375°F/Gas Mark 5, for 15-20 minutes.

7 Remove the tomatoes from the oven and allow to cool until just warm.

8 Arrange the pasta-stuffed tomatoes on a serving dish, garnish with the basil sprigs and serve.

# Venison meatballs

The sharp, citrus-like flavour of kumquats is the perfect complement to these tasty steamed meatballs. Serve with pasta and fresh vegetables.

## NUTRITIONAL INFORMATION

Calories ...... 181    Sugars ........ 8g
Protein ....... 26g    Fat .......... 2g
Carbohydrate ... 11g   Saturates ...... 1g

 5–10 mins     10 mins

### SERVES 4

## INGREDIENTS

450 g/1 lb lean minced venison

1 small leek, finely chopped

1 medium carrot, finely grated

½ tsp ground nutmeg

1 medium egg white, lightly beaten

salt and pepper

### SAUCE

100 g/3½ oz kumquats

1 tbsp caster sugar

150 ml/5 fl oz water

4 tbsp dry sherry

1 tsp cornflour

### TO SERVE

freshly cooked pasta or noodles

freshly cooked vegetables

1 Place the venison in a mixing bowl together with the leek, carrot, seasoning and nutmeg. Add the egg white and bind the ingredients together with your hands until the mixture is well moulded and firm.

2 Divide the mixture into 16 equal portions. Using your fingers, form each portion into a small round ball.

3 Bring a large pan of water to the boil. Arrange the meatballs on a layer of baking paper in a steamer and place over the boiling water. Cover and steam for 10 minutes until cooked through.

4 Meanwhile, wash and thinly slice the kumquats. Place them in a saucepan with the sugar and water and bring to the boil. Simmer for 2–3 minutes until tender.

5 Blend the sherry and cornflour together and add to the pan. Heat through, stirring, until the kumquat sauce thickens. Season to taste.

6 Drain the meatballs and transfer to a serving plate. Spoon over the sauce and serve with pasta and vegetables.

# Chicken & Spinach Lasagne

A delicious pasta bake with all the colours of the Italian flag – red tomatoes, green spinach and pasta, and white chicken and sauce.

## NUTRITIONAL INFORMATION

Calories ...... 358  Sugars ....... 12g
Protein ....... 42g  Fat ........... 9g
Carbohydrate .. 22g  Saturates ...... 4g

25 mins  |  50 mins

### SERVES 4

## INGREDIENTS

350 g/12 oz frozen chopped spinach, defrosted and drained

½ tsp ground nutmeg

450 g/1 lb lean, cooked chicken meat, skinned and diced

4 sheets no-pre-cook lasagne verde

1½ tbsp cornflour

425 ml/15 fl oz skimmed milk

70 g/2½ oz freshly grated Parmesan cheese

### TOMATO SAUCE

400 g/14 oz canned chopped tomatoes

1 onion, finely chopped

1 garlic clove, crushed

150 ml/5 fl oz white wine

3 tbsp tomato purée

1 tsp dried oregano

salt and pepper

green salad, to serve

2 Drain the defrosted spinach again and spread it out on kitchen paper to make sure that as much water as possible is removed. Layer the spinach across the base of an ovenproof baking dish. Sprinkle with the ground nutmeg and season with salt and pepper to taste.

3 Arrange the diced chicken over the spinach and spoon over the tomato sauce. Arrange the sheets of lasagne over the tomato sauce layer.

4 Blend the cornflour with a little of the milk to make a paste. Pour the remaining milk into a saucepan and stir in the cornflour paste. Heat for 2–3 minutes, stirring constantly, until the sauce thickens. Season with salt and pepper.

5 Spoon the sauce over the lasagne and transfer the dish to a baking tray. Sprinkle the grated cheese over the sauce and bake in the oven for 25 minutes until golden brown. Serve with a green salad.

1 Preheat the oven to 200°C/400°F/Gas Mark 6. For the tomato sauce, place the tomatoes in a saucepan and stir in the onion, garlic, wine, tomato purée and oregano. Bring to the boil and simmer for 20 minutes until thick. Season well.

# Chicken & Tomato Lasagne

This variation of the traditional beef dish has layers of pasta and chicken or turkey baked in red wine, tomatoes and a delicious cheese sauce.

## NUTRITIONAL INFORMATION

Calories . . . . . . 550   Sugars . . . . . . . 11g
Protein . . . . . . . 35g   Fat . . . . . . . . . . 29g
Carbohydrate . . 34g   Saturates . . . . . 12g

   20 mins      1¼ hrs

### SERVES 4

## I N G R E D I E N T S

350 g/12 oz fresh lasagne or 150 g/5½ oz
    dried lasagne (about 9 sheets)

1 tbsp olive oil

1 red onion, finely chopped

1 garlic clove, crushed

100 g/3½ oz mushrooms, wiped and sliced

350 g/12 oz chicken or turkey breast, cut
    into chunks

150 ml/5 fl oz red wine, diluted with
    100 ml/3½ fl oz water

250 g/9 oz passata

1 tsp sugar

### B É C H A M E L   S A U C E

5 tbsp butter

6 tbsp plain flour

600 ml/1 pint milk

1 egg, beaten

75 g/2¾ oz freshly grated Parmesan cheese

salt and pepper

1 Cook the lasagne according to the instructions on the packet. Lightly grease a deep ovenproof dish.

2 Heat the oil in a pan. Add the onion and garlic and cook for 3–4 minutes. Add the mushrooms and chicken and stir-fry for 4 minutes or until the meat browns.

3 Add the wine, bring to the boil, then simmer for 5 minutes. Stir in the passata and sugar and cook for 3–5 minutes until the meat is tender and cooked through. The sauce should have thickened, but still be quite runny.

4 To make the Béchamel Sauce, melt the butter in a pan, stir in the flour and cook for 2 minutes. Remove the pan from the heat and gradually add the milk, mixing to form a smooth sauce. Return the pan to the heat and bring to the boil, stirring until thickened. Leave to cool slightly, then beat in the egg and half of the cheese. Season to taste.

5 Place 3 sheets of lasagne in the base of the dish and spread with half of the chicken mixture. Repeat the layers. Top with the last 3 sheets of lasagne, pour over the Béchamel Sauce and sprinkle with the Parmesan cheese. Bake in a preheated oven, 190°C/375°F/Gas Mark 5, for 30 minutes, until golden and the pasta is cooked.

# Smoked Haddock Casserole

This quick, easy and inexpensive dish would be ideal for a mid-week family supper.

## NUTRITIONAL INFORMATION

Calories . . . . . . .525   Sugars . . . . . . . . .8g
Protein . . . . . . . .41g   Fat . . . . . . . . . .18g
Carbohydrate . . .53g   Saturates . . . . . .10g

20 mins       45 mins

### SERVES 4

## INGREDIENTS

2 tbsp butter, plus extra for greasing

450 g/1 lb smoked haddock fillets,
    cut into 4 slices

600 ml/1 pint milk

2 tbsp plain flour

pinch of freshly grated nutmeg

3 tbsp double cream

1 tbsp chopped fresh parsley

2 eggs, hard-boiled and mashed to a pulp

450 g/1 lb dried fusilli

1 tbsp lemon juice

salt and pepper

boiled new potatoes and beetroot, to serve

1 Thoroughly grease a casserole with butter. Put the haddock in the casserole and pour over the milk. Bake in a preheated oven, 200°C/400°F/Gas Mark 6, for about 15 minutes. Carefully pour the cooking liquid into a jug without breaking up the fish.

2 Melt the 2 tablespoons of butter in a saucepan and stir in the flour. Gradually whisk in the reserved cooking liquid. Season to taste with salt, pepper and nutmeg. Stir in the cream, parsley and mashed egg and cook, stirring constantly, for 2 minutes.

3 Meanwhile, bring a large saucepan of lightly salted water to the boil. Add the fusilli and lemon juice and cook for 8-10 minutes until tender, but still firm to the bite.

4 Drain the pasta and spoon or tip it over the fish. Top with the egg sauce and return the casserole to the oven for a further 10 minutes.

5 Serve the fish casserole with boiled new potatoes and freshly cooked beetroot.

## VARIATION
You can use any type of dried pasta for this casserole. Try penne, conchiglie or rigatoni.

# Sea Bass with Olive Sauce

A favourite fish for chefs, the delicious sea bass is now becoming increasingly common in supermarkets and fishmongers for family meals.

## NUTRITIONAL INFORMATION

Calories . . . . . . 877   Sugars . . . . . . . . 3g
Protein . . . . . . . 50g   Fat . . . . . . . . . . 47g
Carbohydrate . . 67g   Saturates . . . . . 26g

10 mins     30 mins

### SERVES 4

## I N G R E D I E N T S

450 g/1 lb dried macaroni

1 tbsp olive oil

8 x 115 g/4 oz sea bass medallions

### S A U C E

2 tbsp butter

4 shallots, chopped

2 tbsp capers

175 g/6 oz stoned green olives, chopped

4 tbsp balsamic vinegar

300 ml/10 fl oz fish stock

300 ml/10 fl oz double cream

juice of 1 lemon

salt and pepper

### T O   G A R N I S H

lemon slices

shredded leek

shredded carrot

1 To make the sauce, melt the butter in a frying pan. Add the shallots and cook gently over a low heat for 4 minutes. Add the capers and chopped olives and cook for a further 3 minutes.

2 Stir in the balsamic vinegar and fish stock, bring to the boil and reduce by half. Add the cream, stirring, and reduce again by half. Season to taste with salt and pepper and stir in the lemon juice. Remove the pan from the heat, set aside and keep warm.

3 Bring a large pan of lightly salted water to the boil. Add the pasta and olive oil and cook for about 12 minutes, or until tender but still firm to the bite.

4 Meanwhile, lightly grill the sea bass medallions for 3–4 minutes on each side, until cooked through, but still moist and delicate.

5 Drain the pasta thoroughly and transfer to large individual serving dishes. Top the pasta with the fish medallions and pour over the olive sauce. Garnish the sea bass with lemon slices, shredded leek and shredded carrot and serve immediately.

# Spaghetti alla Bucaniera

Brill was once known as poor man's turbot, an unfair description as it is a delicately flavoured and delicious fish in its own right.

## NUTRITIONAL INFORMATION

| | | | |
|---|---|---|---|
| Calories | 588 | Sugars | 5g |
| Protein | 36g | Fat | 18g |
| Carbohydrate | 68g | Saturates | 9g |

 25 mins    50 mins

### SERVES 4

## I N G R E D I E N T S

90 g/3 oz plain flour

450 g/1 lb brill or sole fillets, skinned and chopped

450 g/1 lb hake fillets, skinned and chopped

6 tbsp butter

4 shallots, finely chopped

2 garlic cloves, crushed

1 carrot, diced

1 leek, finely chopped

300 ml/10 fl oz dry cider

300 ml/10 fl oz medium sweet cider

2 tsp anchovy essence

1 tbsp tarragon vinegar

450 g/1 lb dried spaghetti

1 tbsp olive oil

salt and pepper

chopped fresh parsley, to garnish

warm crusty brown bread, to serve

1 Season the flour with salt and pepper. Sprinkle 3 tablespoons of the seasoned flour onto a shallow plate. Press the fish pieces into the seasoned flour until they are thoroughly coated.

2 Melt the butter in a flameproof casserole. Add the fish fillets, shallots, garlic, carrot and leek and cook over a low heat, stirring frequently, for about 10 minutes.

3 Sprinkle over the remaining seasoned flour and cook, stirring constantly, for 2 minutes. Gradually stir in the cider, anchovy essence and tarragon vinegar. Bring the mixture to the boil and simmer over a low heat for 35 minutes. Alternatively, bake in a preheated oven, 180°C/350°F/Gas Mark 4, for 30 minutes.

4 About 15 minutes before the end of the cooking time, bring a large pan of lightly salted water to the boil. Add the spaghetti and olive oil and cook for about 12 minutes, or until tender but still firm to the bite. Drain the pasta thoroughly and transfer to a large serving dish.

5 Arrange the fish on top of the spaghetti and pour over the sauce. Garnish with chopped parsley and serve immediately with warm, crusty brown bread.

# Fillets of Red Mullet & Pasta

A lemon and herb sauce perfectly complements the sweet flavour and delicate texture of the fish.

## NUTRITIONAL INFORMATION

| | | | |
|---|---|---|---|
| Calories . . . . . . 457 | Sugars . . . . . . . . 3g |
| Protein . . . . . . . 39g | Fat . . . . . . . . . . 12g |
| Carbohydrate . . 44g | Saturates . . . . . . 5g |

 15 mins    1 hr

### SERVES 4

## I N G R E D I E N T S

1 kg/2 lb 4 oz red mullet fillets

300 ml/10 fl oz dry white wine

4 shallots, finely chopped

1 garlic clove, crushed

3 tbsp finely chopped mixed fresh herbs

finely grated rind and juice of 1 lemon

pinch of freshly grated nutmeg

3 anchovy fillets, roughly chopped

1 tbsp butter

2 tbsp double cream

1 tsp cornflour

450 g/1 lb dried vermicelli

1 tbsp olive oil

salt and pepper

### TO GARNISH

1 fresh mint sprig

lemon slices

lemon rind

1 Put the red mullet fillets in a large casserole. Pour the wine over them and add half the chopped shallots with the garlic, herbs, lemon rind and juice, nutmeg and anchovies. Season. Cover the casserole and bake in a preheated oven, 180°C/350°F/Gas Mark 4, for 35 minutes.

2 Transfer the baked mullet carefully to a warm plate. Set the plate aside and keep warm.

3 Heat the butter in a pan and cook the remaining shallots over a low heat, stirring, for 5 minutes. Pour the cooking liquid into the pan and bring to the boil. Simmer for 25 minutes, until reduced by half. Mix the cream and cornflour and stir into the sauce to thicken.

4 Meanwhile, bring a pan of lightly salted water to the boil. Add the vermicelli and oil and cook for 8–10 minutes, or until tender but still firm to the bite. Drain the pasta and transfer to a warm serving dish.

5 Arrange the red mullet fillets on top of the vermicelli and pour over the sauce. Garnish with a mint sprig, slices of lemon and strips of lemon rind and serve immediately.

# Spaghetti al Tonno

The classic Italian combination of pasta and tuna is enhanced in this recipe with a delicious parsley sauce.

## NUTRITIONAL INFORMATION

Calories . . . . . 1065   Sugars . . . . . . . . 3g
Protein . . . . . . . 27g   Fat . . . . . . . . . . 85g
Carbohydrate . . 52g   Saturates . . . . . 18g

10 mins     15 mins

### SERVES 4

## I N G R E D I E N T S

200 g/7 oz can tuna, drained

60 g/2 oz can anchovies, drained

250 ml/9 fl oz olive oil

60 g/2 oz roughly chopped flat leaf parsley

150 ml/5 fl oz crème fraîche

450 g/1 lb dried spaghetti

2 tbsp butter

salt and pepper

black olives, to garnish

warm crusty bread, to serve

1 Remove any bones from the tuna meat. Put the tuna into a food processor or blender, together with the anchovies, 225 ml/8 fl oz of the olive oil and the flat-leaved parsley. Process until the sauce is very smooth.

2 Spoon the crème fraîche into the food processor or blender and process again for a few seconds to blend thoroughly. Season with salt and pepper to taste.

3 Bring a large pan of lightly salted water to the boil. Add the dried spaghetti and the remaining olive oil and cook for 8–10 minutes, or until tender, but still firm to the bite.

4 Drain the spaghetti, return to the pan and place over a medium heat. Add the butter and toss well to coat. Spoon in the sauce and quickly toss into the spaghetti, mixing well, using 2 forks.

5 Remove the pan from the heat, divide the spaghetti into portions and transfer onto warmed plates. Garnish each portion with olives and serve immediately with warm, crusty bread.

## VARIATION

If liked, you could add 1–2 garlic cloves to the sauce, substitute 25 g/1 oz chopped fresh basil for half the parsley and garnish with capers instead of black olives.

# Poached Salmon with Penne

Fresh salmon and pasta in a mouthwatering lemon and watercress sauce – a wonderful summer evening treat.

## NUTRITIONAL INFORMATION

Calories  . . . . . . 968    Sugars  . . . . . . . . 3g
Protein  . . . . . . . 59g    Fat  . . . . . . . . . . 58g
Carbohydrate  . . 49g    Saturates  . . . . . 19g

  10 mins      30 mins

### SERVES 4

## I N G R E D I E N T S

4 x 275 g/9½ oz fresh salmon steaks

4 tbsp butter

175 ml/6 fl oz dry white wine

sea salt

8 peppercorns

fresh dill sprig

fresh tarragon sprig

1 lemon, sliced

450 g/1 lb dried penne

2 tbsp olive oil

lemon slices and fresh watercress,
  to garnish

### L E M O N   S A U C E

2 tbsp butter

3 tbsp plain flour

150 ml/5 fl oz warm milk

juice and finely grated rind of 2 lemons

60 g/2 oz watercress or young spinach
  leaves, chopped, plus extra to garnish

salt and pepper

1 Place the salmon in a large, non-stick pan. Add the butter, white wine, a pinch of sea salt, the peppercorns, dill, tarragon and lemon. Cover, bring to the boil, and simmer for 10 minutes.

2 Using a fish slice, carefully remove the salmon. Strain and reserve the cooking liquid. Remove and discard the salmon skin and centre bones. Place on a warm dish, cover and keep warm.

3 Meanwhile, bring a saucepan of salted water to the boil. Add the penne and 1 tablespoon of the oil and cook for 8–10 minutes, or until tender, but still firm to the bite. Drain and sprinkle over the remaining olive oil. Place on a warm serving dish, top with the salmon steaks and keep warm.

4 To make the sauce, melt the butter and stir in the flour for 2 minutes. Stir in the milk and about 7 tablespoons of the reserved cooking liquid. Add the lemon juice and rind and cook, stirring, for a further 10 minutes.

5 Add the watercress or spinach to the sauce, stir gently and season to taste with salt and pepper.

6 Pour the sauce over the salmon and penne, garnish with slices of lemon and fresh watercress and serve.

# Trout with Smoked Bacon

Most trout available nowadays is farmed rainbow trout. However, if you can, buy wild brown trout for this recipe.

## NUTRITIONAL INFORMATION

| | | | |
|---|---|---|---|
| Calories | . . . . . . 802 | Sugars | . . . . . . . . 8g |
| Protein | . . . . . . . 68g | Fat | . . . . . . . . . . 36g |
| Carbohydrate | . . 54g | Saturates | . . . . . 10g |

 35 mins     25 mins

### SERVES 4

## I N G R E D I E N T S

butter, for greasing

4 x 275 g/9½ oz trout, gutted and cleaned

12 anchovies in oil, drained and chopped

2 apples, peeled, cored and sliced

4 fresh mint sprigs

juice of 1 lemon

12 slices rindless smoked fatty bacon

450 g/1 lb dried tagliatelle

1 tbsp olive oil

salt and pepper

### TO GARNISH

2 apples, cored and sliced

4 fresh mint sprigs

1 Grease a deep baking tray with plenty of butter. Set aside.

2 Open up the cavities of each trout and rinse with warm salt water.

3 Season each cavity with salt and pepper. Divide the anchovies, sliced apple and mint sprigs between the cavities. Sprinkle lemon juice into each cavity.

4 Carefully cover the whole of each trout, except the head and tail, with three slices of smoked bacon in a spiral.

5 Arrange the stuffed trout on the baking tray with the loose ends of bacon tucked underneath. Season the fish with pepper and bake in a preheated oven, 200°C/400°F/Gas Mark 6, for 20 minutes, turning the trout over after 10 minutes to cook them evenly.

6 Meanwhile, bring a large pan of lightly salted water to the boil. Add the tagliatelle and olive oil and cook for about 12 minutes, or until tender but still firm to the bite. Drain the pasta and transfer to a large, warm serving dish.

7 Remove the trout from the oven and arrange on the tagliatelle. Garnish with sliced apples and fresh mint sprigs and serve immediately.

# Seafood Lasagne

You can use any fish and any sauce you like in this recipe: try smoked finnan haddock and whisky sauce or cod with cheese sauce.

## NUTRITIONAL INFORMATION

Calories ...... 790     Sugars ....... 23g
Protein ....... 55g     Fat .......... 32g
Carbohydrate .. 74g     Saturates ..... 19g

30 mins        45 mins

### SERVES 4

## INGREDIENTS

450 g/1 lb finnan haddock, filleted, skin removed and flesh flaked

115 g/ 4 oz prawns

115 g/4 oz sole fillet, skin removed and flesh sliced

juice of 1 lemon

### SAUCE

4 tbsp butter

3 leeks, very thinly sliced

60 g/2 oz plain flour

about 600 ml/1 pint milk

2 tbsp clear honey

200g/7 oz grated mozzarella cheese

450g/1 lb pre-cooked lasagne

60 g/2 oz freshly grated Parmesan cheese

pepper

## VARIATION

For a cider sauce, substitute 1 finely chopped shallot for the leeks, 300 ml/10 fl oz cider and 300 ml/10 fl oz double cream for the milk and 1 teaspoon of mustard for the honey. For a Tuscan sauce, substitute 1 chopped fennel bulb for the leeks; omit the honey.

1 Put the haddock fillet, prawns and sole fillet into a large bowl and season with pepper and lemon juice to taste. Cover the bowl and set it aside while you make the leek and cheese sauce.

2 Melt the butter in a large saucepan. Add the leeks and cook, stirring occasionally, for 8 minutes. Add the flour and cook, stirring constantly, for 1 minute. Gradually stir in enough milk to make a thick, creamy sauce.

3 Blend in the honey and mozzarella cheese and continue cooking for a further 3 minutes. Remove the pan from the heat and mix in the fish and prawns.

4 Make alternate layers of fish sauce and lasagne in an ovenproof dish, finishing with a layer of fish sauce on top. Generously sprinkle over the grated Parmesan cheese and bake in a preheated oven, 180°C/350°F/Gas Mark 4, for 30 minutes. Serve immediately.

# Pasta & Prawn Parcels

This is the ideal dish when you have unexpected guests because the parcels are quick to prepare but look fantastic.

## NUTRITIONAL INFORMATION

Calories ...... 640    Sugars ........ 1g
Protein ....... 50g    Fat .......... 29g
Carbohydrate .. 42g    Saturates ...... 4g

15 mins        30 mins

### SERVES 4

## I N G R E D I E N T S

450 g/1 lb dried fettuccine

150 ml/5 fl oz Pesto Sauce (see page 73)

4 tsp extra virgin olive oil

750 g/1 lb 10 oz large raw prawns,
    peeled and deveined

2 garlic cloves, crushed

125 ml/4 fl oz dry white wine

salt and pepper

1 Cut out four 30cm/12 inch squares of greaseproof paper.

2 Bring a large saucepan of lightly salted water to the boil. Add the fettuccine and cook for 2–3 minutes, until just softened. Drain and set aside.

3 Mix together the fettuccine and half of the Pesto Sauce. Spread out the paper squares and put 1 teaspoon of olive oil in the middle of each. Divide the fettuccine between the the squares, then divide the prawns and place on top of the fettuccine.

4 Mix together the remaining Pesto Sauce and the garlic and spoon it over the prawns. Season each parcel with salt and pepper and sprinkle with the wine.

5 Dampen the edges of the greaseproof paper and wrap the parcels loosely, twisting the edges to seal.

6 Place the parcels on a baking tray and bake them in a preheated oven, 200°C/400°F/ Gas Mark 6, for 10–15 minutes. Transfer the parcels to individual serving plates and serve immediately.

## COOK'S TIP

Traditionally, these parcels are designed to look like money bags. The resemblance is more effective with greaseproof paper than with foil.

# Vermicelli with Clams

A quickly cooked recipe that transforms ordinary storecupboard ingredients into a dish with style.

## NUTRITIONAL INFORMATION

| | | |
|---|---|---|
| Calories ...... 520 | Sugars ........ 2g | |
| Protein ....... 26g | Fat .......... 13g | |
| Carbohydrate .. 71g | Saturates ...... 4g | |

 10 mins  25 mins

### SERVES 4

## INGREDIENTS

400 g/14 oz dried vermicelli, spaghetti or other long pasta

2 tbsp olive oil

2 tbsp butter

2 onions, chopped

2 garlic cloves, chopped

2 x 200 g/7 oz jars clams in brine

125 ml/4 fl oz white wine

4 tbsp chopped fresh parsley

½ tsp dried oregano

pinch of freshly grated nutmeg

2 tbsp Parmesan cheese shavings

salt and pepper

fresh basil sprigs, to garnish

1 Bring a large pan of lightly salted water to the boil. Add the pasta and half of the olive oil and cook for 8–10 minutes, or until tender, but still firm to the bite. Drain, return to the pan and add the butter. Cover the pan, shake well and keep warm.

2 Heat the remaining oil in a pan over a medium heat. Add the onions and fry until they are translucent. Stir in the garlic and cook for 1 minute.

3 Strain and reserve the liquid from 1 jar of clams. Add the liquid to the pan, with the wine. Stir, bring to simmering point and simmer for 3 minutes. Drain the second jar of clams and discard the liquid.

4 Add the clams, parsley and oregano to the pan and season with pepper and nutmeg. Lower the heat and cook until the sauce is heated through.

5 Transfer the pasta to a warm serving dish and pour over the sauce. Sprinkle with the Parmesan cheese, garnish with the basil and serve immediately.

## COOK'S TIP

There are many different types of clams found along almost every coast in the world. Those traditionally used in this dish are the tiny ones, only 2.5–5 cm/1–2 inches across, known in Italy as vongole.

# Broccoli & Anchovy Pasta

Orecchiette, the cup-shaped pasta from southern Italy, is excellent for this filling dish because it scoops up the robust, chunky sauce.

## NUTRITIONAL INFORMATION

| | | | |
|---|---|---|---|
| Calories | 685 | Sugars | 4g |
| Protein | 33g | Fat | 29g |
| Carbohydrate | 78g | Saturates | 9g |

🍅 5 mins     🕒 25 mins

### SERVES 4

## INGREDIENTS

500 g/1 lb 2 oz broccoli

400 g/14 oz dried orecchiette

5 tbsp olive oil

2 large garlic cloves, crushed

50 g/1¾ oz canned anchovy fillets in oil, drained and finely chopped

60 g/2 oz Parmesan cheese, grated

60 g/2 oz pecorino cheese, grated

salt and pepper

1 Bring 2 pans of lightly salted water to the boil. Chop the broccoli florets and stems into small, bite-sized pieces. Add the broccoli to one pan and cook until very tender. Drain and set aside.

2 Put the pasta in the other pan of boiling water and cook for 10–12 minutes or until tender, but still al dente.

3 Meanwhile, heat the olive oil in a large pan over a medium heat. Add the garlic and fry for 3 minutes, stirring, without allowing it to brown. Add the chopped anchovies and cook for 3 minutes, stirring and mashing with a wooden spoon to break them up. Finely grate the Parmesan and pecorino cheeses.

4 Drain the pasta, add to the pan of anchovies and stir. Add the broccoli and stir to mix.

5 Add the grated Parmesan and pecorino to the pasta and stir constantly over a medium–high heat until the cheeses melt and the pasta and broccoli are coated.

6 Adjust the seasoning to taste – the anchovies and cheeses are salty, so you will only need to add pepper, if anything. Spoon into individual bowls or onto plates and serve immediately.

## VARIATIONS

Add dried chilli flakes to taste with the garlic in step 3. If you have difficulty in finding orecchiette, try using conchiglie instead.

# Pasta with Tuna & Lemon

Fusilli – corkscrew-shaped pasta – is the best shape to use for this recipe because the creamy sauce is absorbed in the twists.

## NUTRITIONAL INFORMATION

| | | |
|---|---|---|
| Calories | ...... 891 | Sugars ........ 6g |
| Protein | ....... 27g | Fat .......... 55g |
| Carbohydrate | .. 77g | Saturates ..... 31g |

 5 mins    15 mins

### SERVES 4

## INGREDIENTS

4 tbsp butter, diced

300 ml/10 fl oz double cream

4 tbsp lemon juice

1 tbsp grated lemon rind

½ tsp anchovy essence

400 g/14 oz dried fusilli

200 g/7 oz canned tuna in olive oil, drained and flaked

salt and pepper

### TO GARNISH

2 tbsp finely chopped fresh parsley

strips of lemon rind

1 Bring a large saucepan of lightly salted water to the boil. Melt the butter in a large frying pan. Stir in the cream and lemon juice and simmer, stirring constantly, for about 2 minutes until the mixture has thickened slightly.

2 Stir in the lemon rind and anchovy essence. Meanwhile, cook the pasta for 10–12 minutes, or according to the instructions on the packet, until tender, but still firm to the bite. Drain well.

3 Add the sauce to the pasta and toss until well coated. Add the tuna and gently toss until well blended but without breaking up the tuna.

4 Season to taste with salt and pepper. Transfer to a serving platter and garnish with the parsley and lemon rind. Grind over some pepper and serve at once.

## VARIATIONS

For a vegetarian version, omit the tuna and anchovy essence. Add 150 g/5 oz stoned olives instead. For extra 'kick' add a pinch of dried chilli flakes to the sauce instead of the anchovy essence.

# Sicilian Tagliatelle

This recipe is based on a Sicilian dish combining broccoli and anchovies, but it includes lemon and garlic for more flavour.

## NUTRITIONAL INFORMATION

| | | | |
|---|---|---|---|
| Calories | ...... 529 | Sugars | ........ 4g |
| Protein | ....... 17g | Fat | .......... 20g |
| Carbohydrate | .. 75g | Saturates | ...... 3g |

5 mins    10–15 mins

### SERVES 4

## I N G R E D I E N T S

6 tbsp olive oil

4 tbsp fresh white breadcrumbs

450g/1 lb broccoli, cut into small florets

350 g/12 oz dried tagliatelle

4 anchovy fillets, drained and chopped

2 garlic cloves, sliced

grated rind 1 lemon

large pinch of chilli flakes

salt and pepper

freshly grated Parmesan cheese, to serve

1 Heat 2 tablespoons of the olive oil in a frying pan and add the breadcrumbs. Stir-fry over a medium heat for 4–5 minutes until golden and crisp. Remove from the pan and drain on paper towels.

2 Bring a large pan of salted water to the boil and add the broccoli. Blanch for 3 minutes then drain, reserving the water. Refresh the broccoli under cold water and drain again. Pat dry with kitchen paper and then set aside.

3 Bring the water back to the boil and add the tagliatelle. Cook according to the packet instructions, until tender but still firm to the bite.

4 Meanwhile, heat another 2 tablespoons of the olive oil in a large frying pan or wok and add the chopped anchovies. Cook for 1 minute, then mash with a wooden spoon to a paste. Add the sliced garlic, grated lemon rind and chilli flakes and cook gently for 2 minutes. Add the broccoli and cook for a further 3–4 minutes until heated through.

5 Drain the cooked pasta and add to the broccoli mixture with the remaining 2 tablespoons of olive oil and seasoning. Toss together well.

6 Divide the pasta between individual serving plates. Top with the fried breadcrumbs and grated Parmesan cheese and serve immediately.

# Linguine with Sardines

This is a very quick dish that is ideal for mid-week suppers, as it is simple to prepare but full of flavour.

## NUTRITIONAL INFORMATION

| | | | |
|---|---|---|---|
| Calories | 547 | Sugars | 5g |
| Protein | 23g | Fat | 23g |
| Carbohydrate | 68g | Saturates | 3g |

 5–10 mins    10–15 mins

### SERVES 4

## INGREDIENTS

8 sardines, filleted

1 fennel bulb

4 tbsp olive oil

3 garlic cloves, sliced

1 tsp chilli flakes

350 g/12 oz dried linguine

½ tsp finely grated lemon rind

1 tbsp lemon juice

2 tbsp pine kernels, toasted

2 tbsp chopped fresh parsley, plus extra for garnish

salt and pepper

1 Wash and dry the sardines. Roughly chop into large pieces and set aside. Trim the fennel bulb, removing any tough outer leaves, and slice very thinly.

2 Heat 2 tablespoons of the olive oil in a large frying pan and add the garlic and chilli flakes. Cook for 1 minute then add the fennel. Cook over a medium-high heat for 4–5 minutes until softened. Add the sardine pieces and heat for a further 3–4 minutes until just cooked.

3 Meanwhile, cook the pasta in plenty of boiling salted water according to the packet instructions, until tender but still firm to the bite. Drain well and return to the pan to keep warm.

4 Add the lemon rind and juice, pine kernels, parsley and seasoning to the sardines and toss together. Add to the pasta with the remaining olive oil and toss together gently. Serve immediately with a sprinkling of parsley.

## COOK'S TIP

Reserve a couple of tablespoons of the pasta cooking water and add to the pasta with the sauce if the mixture seems a little dry.

# Spaghettini with Crab

This dish is probably one of the simplest in the book, yet the flavour is as impressive as a recipe over which you have slaved for hours.

## NUTRITIONAL INFORMATION

| | | | |
|---|---|---|---|
| Calories | 488 | Sugars | 3g |
| Protein | 13g | Fat | 19g |
| Carbohydrate | 65g | Saturates | 3g |

 5 mins    5 mins

### SERVES 4

## I N G R E D I E N T S

1 dressed crab, about 450 g/1 lb including the shell

350 g/12 oz dried spaghettini

6 tbsp best quality extra virgin olive oil

1 hot red chilli, deseeded and finely chopped

2 garlic cloves, finely chopped

3 tbsp chopped fresh parsley

1 tsp finely grated lemon rind

2 tbsp lemon juice

salt and pepper

lemon wedges, to garnish

1 Scoop the meat from the crab shell into a bowl. Mix the white and brown meat lightly together and set aside.

2 Bring a large saucepan of salted water to the boil and add the spaghettini. Cook according to the instructions on the packet until tender, but still firm to the bite. Drain well and return to the pan.

3 Meanwhile, heat 2 tablespoons of the olive oil in a frying pan. When hot, add the chilli and garlic. Cook for 30 seconds, then add the crab meat, parsley and lemon rind and juice. Stir-fry for a further minute until the crab is just heated through.

4 Add the crab mixture to the pasta with the remaining olive oil, season to taste and toss together thoroughly. Serve immediately, garnished with lemon wedges.

# Vegetables & Tofu

This is a simple, clean-tasting dish of green vegetables, tofu and pasta, lightly tossed in olive oil.

## NUTRITIONAL INFORMATION

| | |
|---|---|
| Calories . . . . . . 400 | Sugars . . . . . . . . 5g |
| Protein . . . . . . . 19g | Fat . . . . . . . . . . 17g |
| Carbohydrate . . 46g | Saturates . . . . . . 5g |

 25 mins      20 mins

### SERVES 4

## I N G R E D I E N T S

225 g/8 oz asparagus

125 g/4½ oz mangetouts

225 g/8 oz French beans

1 leek

225 g/8 oz shelled small broad beans

300 g/10½ oz dried fusilli

2 tbsp olive oil

2 tbsp butter or margarine

1 garlic clove, crushed

225 g/8 oz tofu, cut into
  2.5 cm/1 inch cubes

60 g/2 oz stoned green olives in
  brine, drained

salt and pepper

freshly grated Parmesan cheese, to serve

1 Cut the asparagus into 5 cm/2 inch lengths. Finely slice the mangetouts diagonally and slice the French beans into 2.5 cm/1 inch pieces. Finely slice the leek.

2 Bring a large saucepan of water to the boil and add the asparagus, French beans and broad beans. Bring back to the boil and cook for 4 minutes until just tender. Drain well and rinse in cold water.

3 Bring a large saucepan of salted water to the boil and cook the fusilli for 8–9 minutes, until just tender. Drain well. Toss in 1 tablespoon of the oil and season well.

4 Meanwhile, in a wok or large frying pan, heat the remaining oil and the butter or margarine and gently fry the leek, garlic and tofu for 1–2 minutes, until the vegetables have just softened.

5 Stir in the mangetouts and continue cooking for 1 minute.

6 Add the boiled vegetables and olives to the pan and heat through for an additional minute. Carefully stir in the pasta and add seasoning. Cook for 1 more minute and then pile into a warmed serving dish. Serve while still hot, sprinkled with grated Parmesan cheese.

# Pasta with Nuts & Cheese

Simple and inexpensive, this tasty and nutritious pasta dish can be prepared fairly quickly.

## NUTRITIONAL INFORMATION

Calories ...... 750    Sugars ........ 6g
Protein ....... 23g    Fat .......... 44g
Carbohydrate .. 70g    Saturates ..... 21g

10 mins    30 mins

### SERVES 4

### INGREDIENTS

60 g/2 oz pine kernels

350 g/12 oz dried pasta shapes

2 courgettes, sliced

125 g/4½ oz broccoli, broken into florets

200 g/7 oz full-fat soft cheese

150 ml/5 fl oz milk

1 tbsp chopped fresh basil

125 g/4½ oz button mushrooms, sliced

90 g/3 oz blue cheese, crumbled

salt and pepper

fresh basil sprigs, to garnish

green salad, to serve

1 Scatter the pine kernels onto a baking tray and grill, turning occasionally, until lightly browned all over. Set aside.

2 Cook the pasta in a large pan of boiling salted water for 8–10 minutes, or until just tender and still al dente – or firm to the bite.

3 Meanwhile, cook the courgettes and broccoli in a small amount of boiling, lightly salted water for about 5 minutes or until just tender.

4 Put the soft cheese into a pan and heat gently, stirring. Add the milk and stir to mix. Add the chopped basil and mushrooms and cook gently for 2–3 minutes. Stir the blue cheese into the mixture and season to taste.

5 Drain the pasta and the vegetables and mix together. Pour the cheese and mushroom sauce over them and add the pine kernels, tossing the pasta gently to mix them in. Garnish with basil sprigs and serve with a green salad.

# Pasta Provençale

A Mediterranean mixture of red peppers, garlic and courgettes cooked in olive oil and tossed with pasta spirals.

## NUTRITIONAL INFORMATION

Calories ...... 487  Sugars ....... 14g
Protein ....... 17g  Fat .......... 24g
Carbohydrate .. 53g  Saturates ...... 8g

5 mins     20 mins

### SERVES 4

## INGREDIENTS

3 tbsp olive oil

1 onion, sliced

2 garlic cloves, chopped

3 red peppers, deseeded and cut into strips

3 courgettes, sliced

400 g/14 oz canned chopped tomatoes

3 tbsp sun-dried tomato paste

2 tbsp chopped fresh basil

225 g/8 oz fresh fusilli

125 g/4½ oz grated Gruyère cheese

salt and pepper

fresh basil sprigs, to garnish

1 Heat the oil in a heavy-based saucepan or flameproof casserole. Add the onion and garlic and cook, stirring occasionally, until softened. Add the peppers and courgettes and fry, stirring occasionally, for 5 minutes.

2 Add the tomatoes, sun-dried tomato paste and basil and season to taste with salt and pepper. Cover and cook for a further 5 minutes.

3 Meanwhile, bring a large saucepan of salted water to the boil and add the pasta. Stir and bring back to the boil. Reduce the heat slightly and cook, uncovered, for 3 minutes, until just tender. Drain thoroughly and add to the vegetable mixture. Toss gently to mix well.

4 Transfer to a shallow flameproof dish and sprinkle with the cheese.

5 Cook under a preheated grill for 5 minutes, until the cheese is golden brown and bubbling. Garnish with basil sprigs and serve immediately.

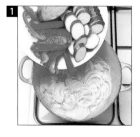

# Vegetable Pasta Nests

These large pasta nests look impressive when presented filled with grilled mixed vegetables, and taste delicious.

## NUTRITIONAL INFORMATION

| | | |
|---|---|---|
| Calories ...... 392 | Sugars ........ 1g | |
| Protein ........ 6g | Fat .......... 28g | |
| Carbohydrate .. 32g | Saturates ...... 9g | |

 25 mins     40 mins

### SERVES 4

### INGREDIENTS

175 g/6 oz spaghetti

1 aubergine, halved and sliced

1 courgette, diced

1 red pepper, deseeded and chopped diagonally

6 tbsp olive oil

2 garlic cloves, crushed

4 tbsp butter or margarine, melted

1 tbsp dry white breadcrumbs

salt and pepper

fresh parsley sprigs, to garnish

1 Bring a large saucepan of water to the boil and cook the spaghetti for 8–10 minutes, or until tender, but still firm to the bite. Drain the spaghetti in a colander and set aside until required.

2 Place the aubergine, courgette and pepper on a baking tray. Mix the oil and garlic together and pour over the vegetables, tossing to coat all over.

3 Cook the vegetables under a preheated hot grill for about 10 minutes, turning, until tender and lightly charred. Set aside and keep warm.

4 Divide the spaghetti among 4 lightly greased Yorkshire pudding tins. Using 2 forks, curl the spaghetti to form nests.

5 Brush the pasta nests with melted butter or margarine and sprinkle with the breadcrumbs. Bake in a preheated oven, 200°C/400°F/Gas Mark 6, for 15 minutes or until lightly golden. Remove the pasta nests from the tins and transfer to serving plates. Divide the grilled vegetables between the nests, season and garnish.

# Basil & Tomato Pasta

Roasting the tomatoes gives a sweeter flavour to this sauce. Buy Italian tomatoes, such as plum or flavia, as these have a better flavour and colour.

## NUTRITIONAL INFORMATION

| | | |
|---|---|---|
| Calories . . . . . . 177 | Sugars . . . . . . . . 4g |
| Protein . . . . . . . . 5g | Fat . . . . . . . . . . . 4g |
| Carbohydrate . . 31g | Saturates . . . . . . 1g |

 15 mins    35 mins

### SERVES 4

## I N G R E D I E N T S

1 tbsp olive oil

2 rosemary sprigs

2 garlic cloves

450 g/1 lb tomatoes, halved

1 tbsp sun-dried tomato paste

12 fresh basil leaves, plus extra to garnish

salt and pepper

675 g/1½ lb fresh farfalle or 350 g/12 oz
    dried farfalle

1 Place the oil, rosemary, garlic and tomatoes, skin side up, in a shallow roasting tin.

2 Drizzle with a little olive oil and cook under a preheated grill for 20 minutes, or until the tomato skins become slightly charred.

3 Peel the skin from the tomatoes. Roughly chop the tomato flesh and place in a pan.

4 Squeeze the pulp from the garlic cloves and mix with the tomato flesh and sun-dried tomato paste.

5 Roughly tear the fresh basil leaves into smaller pieces, then stir them into the sauce. Season with a little salt and pepper to taste. Set aside.

6 Cook the farfalle in a saucepan of boiling water for 8–10 minutes, or until tender, but still firm to the bite. Drain the pasta thoroughly.

7 Gently reheat the tomato and basil sauce, stirring constantly. Take care not to overheat.

8 Transfer the farfalle to serving plates and pour over the basil and tomato sauce. Serve immediately.

## COOK'S TIP

This sauce tastes just as good when served cold in a pasta salad.

# Spinach & Nut Pasta

Use any pasta shapes that you have for this recipe. Multi-coloured tricolore pasta is visually the most attractive.

## NUTRITIONAL INFORMATION

| | | | |
|---|---|---|---|
| Calories | 603 | Sugars | 5g |
| Protein | 12g | Fat | 41g |
| Carbohydrate | 46g | Saturates | 6g |

🧊 5 mins    🕐 15 mins

### SERVES 4

## INGREDIENTS

225 g/8 oz dried pasta

125 ml/4 fl oz olive oil

2 garlic cloves, crushed

1 onion, quartered and sliced

3 large flat mushrooms, sliced

225 g/8 oz spinach

2 tbsp pine kernels

75 ml/3 fl oz dry white wine

salt and pepper

Parmesan cheese shavings, to garnish

1 Cook the pasta in a saucepan of boiling salted water for 8–10 minutes, or until tender, but still firm to the bite. Drain well.

2 Meanwhile, heat the oil in a large saucepan and sauté the garlic and onion for 1 minute.

3 Add the sliced mushrooms to the pan and cook over a medium heat, stirring occasionally, for 2 minutes.

4 Lower the heat, add the spinach to the pan and cook, stirring occasionally, for 4–5 minutes, or until it has wilted.

5 Stir in the pine kernels and wine, season to taste and cook for 1 minute.

6 Transfer the pasta to a warm serving bowl and toss the sauce into it, mixing well. Garnish with shavings of Parmesan cheese and serve.

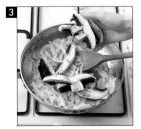

### COOK'S TIP

Grate a little nutmeg over the dish for extra flavour, as this spice has a particular affinity with spinach.

# Macaroni Cheese & Tomato

This is a really simple, family dish which is inexpensive and easy to prepare and cook. Serve with a salad or fresh green vegetables.

## NUTRITIONAL INFORMATION

| | |
|---|---|
| Calories ...... 592 | Sugars ........ 6g |
| Protein ....... 28g | Fat .......... 29g |
| Carbohydrate .. 57g | Saturates ..... 17g |

 15 mins  35–40 mins

### SERVES 4

## INGREDIENTS

225 g/8 oz dried elbow macaroni

175 g/6 oz grated Cheddar cheese

100 g/3½ oz freshly grated
  Parmesan cheese

4 tbsp fresh white breadcrumbs

1 tbsp chopped basil

1 tbsp butter or margarine, plus extra
  for greasing

### TOMATO SAUCE

1 tbsp olive oil

1 shallot, finely chopped

2 garlic cloves, crushed

500 g/1 lb 2 oz canned chopped tomatoes

1 tbsp chopped basil

salt and pepper

1 To make the tomato sauce, heat the oil in a heavy-based saucepan. Add the shallot and garlic and sauté for 1 minute. Add the tomatoes and basil and season with salt and pepper to taste. Cook over a medium heat, stirring constantly, for 10 minutes.

2 Meanwhile, bring a large saucepan of lightly salted water to the boil and cook the macaroni for 8 minutes, or until tender, but still firm to the bite. Drain thoroughly and set aside.

3 Mix the Cheddar and Parmesan together in a bowl. Grease a deep, ovenproof dish. Spoon one-third of the tomato sauce into the base of the dish, top with one-third of the macaroni and then one-third of the cheeses. Season to taste with salt and pepper. Repeat these layers twice, ending with a layer of grated cheese.

4 Combine the breadcrumbs and basil and sprinkle evenly over the top. Dot the topping with butter or margarine and cook in a preheated oven, 190°C/375°F/Gas Mark 5, for 25 minutes, or until the the topping is golden brown and bubbling. Serve immediately.

# Tagliarini with Gorgonzola

This simple, creamy pasta sauce is a classic Italian recipe. You could use Danish blue cheese instead of the Gorgonzola, if you prefer.

## NUTRITIONAL INFORMATION

| | | | |
|---|---|---|---|
| Calories | .......904 | Sugars | .........4g |
| Protein | ........27g | Fat | ..........53g |
| Carbohydrate | ...83g | Saturates | ......36g |

5 mins          20 mins

### SERVES 4

## I N G R E D I E N T S

2 tbsp butter

225 g/8 oz Gorgonzola cheese, roughly crumbled

150 ml/5 fl oz double cream

2 tbsp dry white wine

1 tsp cornflour

4 fresh sage sprigs, finely chopped

400 g/14 oz dried tagliarini

2 tbsp olive oil

salt and white pepper

1 Melt the butter in a heavy-based pan. Stir in 175 g/6 oz of the cheese and melt, over a low heat, for about 2 minutes.

2 Add the cream, wine and cornflour and beat with a whisk until the ingredients are fully incorporated.

## COOK'S TIP

Gorgonzola is one of the world's oldest veined cheeses and, arguably, its finest. When buying, always check that it is creamy yellow with delicate green veining. Avoid hard or discoloured cheese. It should have a rich, piquant aroma, not a bitter smell.

3 Stir in the sage and season to taste with salt and white pepper. Bring to the boil over a low heat, whisking constantly, until the sauce thickens. Remove from the heat and set aside while you cook the pasta.

4 Bring a large saucepan of lightly salted water to the boil. Add the tagliarini and 1 tablespoon of the olive oil. Cook the pasta for 8-10 minutes or until just tender, drain thoroughly and toss in the remaining olive oil. Transfer the pasta to a serving dish and keep warm.

5 Reheat the sauce over a low heat, whisking constantly. Spoon the Gorgonzola sauce over the tagliarini, generously sprinkle over the remaining cheese and serve immediately.

# Three Cheese Bake

Serve this dish while the cheese is still hot and melted, as cooked cheese turns very rubbery if it is allowed to cool down.

## NUTRITIONAL INFORMATION

| | | | |
|---|---|---|---|
| Calories | 710 | Sugars | 6g |
| Protein | 34g | Fat | 30g |
| Carbohydrate | 80g | Saturates | 16g |

5 mins    1 hr

### SERVES 4

### I N G R E D I E N T S

butter, for greasing

400 g/14 oz dried penne pasta

1 tbsp olive oil

2 eggs, beaten

350 g/12 oz ricotta cheese

4 sprigs fresh basil

100 g/3½ oz mozzarella or halloumi cheese, grated

70 g/2½ oz freshly grated Parmesan cheese

salt and pepper

fresh basil leaves, to garnish (optional)

1 Lightly grease a large ovenproof dish with butter. and set it aside.

2 Bring a large pan of lightly salted water to the boil. Add the penne and olive oil and cook for 8–10 minutes, or until just tender, but still firm to the bite. Drain the pasta, set aside and keep warm.

3 Break the eggs into a bowl and beat lightly together. Beat the eggs into the ricotta cheese and season as required to taste.

4 Spoon half of the penne into the base of the prepared dish and cover with half of the basil leaves.

5 Spoon over half of the ricotta cheese mixture. Sprinkle over the mozzarella or halloumi cheese and top with the remaining basil leaves. Cover with the remaining penne, then spoon over the remaining ricotta cheese mixture. Lightly sprinkle the Parmesan cheese over the top.

6 Bake in a preheated oven, 190°C/375°F/Gas Mark 5, for 30–40 minutes until golden brown and the cheese topping is hot and bubbling. Garnish with fresh basil leaves, if liked, and serve immediately.

## VARIATION

Try substituting smoked Bavarian cheese for the mozzarella or halloumi and grated Cheddar cheese for the Parmesan, for a slightly different but equally delicious flavour.

# Paglia e Fieno

The name of this dish – 'straw and hay' – refers to the colours of the pasta when mixed together.

## NUTRITIONAL INFORMATION

| | | | |
|---|---|---|---|
| Calories | 699 | Sugars | 7g |
| Protein | 26g | Fat | 39g |
| Carbohydrate | 65g | Saturates | 23g |

10 mins     10 mins

### SERVES 4

## INGREDIENTS

4 tbsp butter

450 g/1 lb fresh peas, shelled

200 ml/7 fl oz double cream

450 g/1 lb mixed fresh green and white spaghetti or tagliatelle

1 tbsp olive oil

60 g/2¼ oz freshly grated Parmesan cheese, plus shavings to serve

pinch of freshly grated nutmeg

salt and pepper

1 Melt the butter in a large saucepan. Add the peas and cook, over a low heat, for 2–3 minutes.

2 Using a measuring jug, pour 150 ml/ 5 fl oz of the cream into the pan, bring to the boil and simmer for 1–1½ minutes, or until slightly thickened. Remove the pan from the heat.

3 Meanwhile, bring a large pan of lightly salted water to the boil. Add the spaghetti or tagliatelle and olive oil and cook for 2–3 minutes, or until just tender but still firm to the bite. Remove the pan from the heat, drain the pasta thoroughly and return to the pan.

4 Add the peas and cream sauce to the pasta. Return the pan to the heat and add the remaining cream and the Parmesan cheese and season to taste with salt, pepper and grated nutmeg.

5 Using 2 forks, gently toss the pasta to coat with the peas and cream sauce, while heating through.

6 Transfer the pasta to a serving dish and serve immediately, topped with shavings of Parmesan cheese.

### VARIATION

Fry 140 g/5 oz sliced button or oyster mushrooms in 4 tablespoons of butter over a low heat for 4–5 minutes. Stir into the peas and cream sauce just before adding to the pasta in step 4.

# Green Tagliatelle with Garlic

A rich pasta dish for garlic lovers everywhere. It is quick and easy to prepare and full of flavour.

## NUTRITIONAL INFORMATION

| | |
|---|---|
| Calories ...... 526 | Sugars ........ 3g |
| Protein ....... 14g | Fat .......... 34g |
| Carbohydrate .. 45g | Saturates ..... 13g |

5 mins          20 mins

### SERVES 4

## INGREDIENTS

2 tbsp walnut oil

1 bunch spring onions, sliced

2 garlic cloves, thinly sliced

250 g/8 oz sliced mushrooms

450 g/1 lb fresh green and white tagliatelle

1 tbsp olive oil

225 g/8 oz frozen spinach, defrosted and drained

115 g/4 oz full-fat soft cheese with garlic and herbs

4 tbsp single cream

60 g/2 oz chopped, unsalted pistachio nuts

2 tbsp shredded fresh basil

salt and pepper

### TO GARNISH

fresh basil sprigs

Italian bread, to serve

3 Meanwhile, bring a large saucepan of lightly salted water to the boil. Add the tagliatelle and olive oil and cook for 3–5 minutes, or until tender but still firm to the bite. Drain the tagliatelle thoroughly and return to the saucepan.

4 Add the spinach to the frying pan and heat through for 1–2 minutes. Add the cheese to the pan and allow to melt slightly. Stir in the cream and continue to cook, without allowing the mixture to come to the boil, until warmed through.

5 Pour the sauce over the pasta, season to taste with salt and black pepper and mix well. Heat through gently, stirring constantly, for 2–3 minutes.

6 Transfer the pasta to a serving dish and sprinkle with the pistachio nuts and shredded basil. Garnish with the basil sprigs and serve immediately with the Italian bread of your choice.

1 Heat the walnut oil in a large frying pan. Add the spring onions and garlic and fry for 1 minute, until just softened.

2 Add the mushrooms to the pan, stir well, cover and cook over a low heat for about 5 minutes, until softened.

# Patriotic Pasta

The ingredients of this dish have the same bright colours as the Italian flag – hence its name.

## NUTRITIONAL INFORMATION

| | | |
|---|---|---|
| Calories ...... 325 | Sugars ........ 5g |
| Protein ........ 8g | Fat .......... 13g |
| Carbohydrate .. 48g | Saturates ...... 2g |

 5 mins     15 mins

### SERVES 4

### INGREDIENTS

450 g/1 lb dried farfalle

4 tbsp olive oil

450 g/1 lb cherry tomatoes

90 g/3 oz rocket

salt and pepper

pecorino cheese, to garnish

1 Bring a large saucepan of lightly salted water to the boil. Add the farfalle and 1 tablespoon of the olive oil and cook for 8–10 minutes, or until tender, but still firm to the bite. Drain the farfalle thoroughly and return to the pan.

2 Cut the cherry tomatoes in half and trim the rocket.

3 Heat the remaining olive oil in a large saucepan. Add the tomatoes to the pan and cook for 1 minute. Add the farfalle and rocket to the pan and stir gently to mix together. Heat through and season to taste with salt and pepper.

4 Meanwhile, using a vegetable peeler, shave thin slices of pecorino cheese.

5 Transfer the farfalle and vegetables to a warm serving dish. Garnish with the cheese shavings and serve immediately.

## COOK'S TIP

Pecorino cheese is a hard sheep's milk cheese which resembles Parmesan, and is often used for grating over a variety of dishes. It has a sharp flavour and is only used in small quantities.

# Mediterranean Spaghetti

Delicious Mediterranean vegetables, cooked in rich tomato sauce, make an ideal topping for nutty wholemeal pasta.

## NUTRITIONAL INFORMATION

| Calories | . . . . . . 547 | Sugars | . . . . . . . 19g |
|---|---|---|---|
| Protein | . . . . . . . 16g | Fat | . . . . . . . . . . 16g |
| Carbohydrate | . . 91g | Saturates | . . . . . . 5g |

 5 mins      35 mins

### SERVES 4

## I N G R E D I E N T S

2 tbsp olive oil

1 large red onion, chopped

2 garlic cloves, crushed

1 tbsp lemon juice

4 baby aubergines, quartered

600 ml/1 pint passata

2 tsp caster sugar

2 tbsp tomato purée

400 g/14 oz canned artichoke hearts,
    drained and halved

115 g/4 oz stoned black olives

350 g/12 oz dried spaghetti

2 tbsp butter

salt and pepper

fresh basil sprigs, to garnish

olive bread, to serve

1 Heat 1 tablespoon of the olive oil in a large frying pan. Add the onion, garlic, lemon juice and aubergines and cook over a low heat for 4–5 minutes, until the onion and aubergines are lightly golden brown.

2 Pour in the passata, season to taste with salt and black pepper and stir in the caster sugar and tomato purée. Bring to the boil, lower the heat and then simmer, stirring occasionally, for 20 minutes.

3 Gently stir in the artichoke hearts and black olives and cook for 5 minutes.

4 Meanwhile, bring a large saucepan of lightly salted water to the boil. Add the spaghetti and the remaining oil and cook for 7–8 minutes, or until tender but still firm to the bite.

5 Drain the spaghetti thoroughly, toss with the butter to coat it well and transfer to a large serving dish.

6 Pour the vegetable sauce over the spaghetti, garnish with the sprigs of fresh basil and serve immediately with slices of olive bread.

# Spinach & Mushroom Lasagne

This is one of the tastiest vegetarian dishes. For a variation you could substitute sliced roasted peppers for the spinach (see below).

## NUTRITIONAL INFORMATION

| | | | |
|---|---|---|---|
| Calories | ...... 720 | Sugars | ........ 9g |
| Protein | ....... 31g | Fat | .......... 52g |
| Carbohydrate | ...36g | Saturates | ..... 32g |

20 mins        40 mins

### SERVES 4

## I N G R E D I E N T S

115 g/4 oz butter, plus extra for greasing

2 garlic cloves, finely chopped

115 g/4 oz shallots

225 g/8 oz wild mushrooms, such as chanterelles

450 g/1 lb spinach, cooked, drained and finely chopped

225 g/8 oz grated Cheddar cheese

¼ tsp freshly grated nutmeg

1 tsp chopped fresh basil

60 g/2 oz plain flour

600 ml/1 pint hot milk

60 g/2 oz grated Cheshire cheese

salt and pepper

8 sheets pre-cooked lasagne

1 Lightly grease a large ovenproof dish with a little butter.

2 Melt half of the butter in a saucepan. Add the garlic, shallots and wild mushrooms and fry over a low heat for 3 minutes. Stir in the spinach, Cheddar cheese, nutmeg and basil. Season with salt and pepper to taste and set aside.

3 Melt the remaining butter in another saucepan over a low heat. Add the flour and cook, stirring constantly, for 1 minute. Gradually stir in the hot milk,

whisking constantly until smooth. Stir in 25 g/1 oz of the Cheshire cheese and season to taste with salt and pepper.

4 Spread half of the mushroom and spinach mixture over the base of the prepared dish. Cover with a layer of lasagne, then with half of the cheese sauce. Repeat the process and sprinkle over the remaining Cheshire cheese.

5 Bake in a preheated oven, 200°C/ 400°F/Gas Mark 6, for 30 minutes, or until golden brown. Serve hot.

## VARIATION

You could substitute 4 peppers for the spinach. Roast in a preheated oven, 200°C/400°F/Gas Mark 6, for 20 minutes. Rub off the skins under cold water, deseed and chop before using.

# Spaghetti & Mushroom Sauce

This easy vegetarian dish is ideal for busy people with little time, but plenty of good taste.

## NUTRITIONAL INFORMATION

| | |
|---|---|
| Calories ...... 604 | Sugars ........ 5g |
| Protein ....... 11g | Fat .......... 39g |
| Carbohydrate .. 54g | Saturates ..... 21g |

 20 mins     35 mins

### SERVES 4

## INGREDIENTS

4 tbsp butter

2 tbsp olive oil

6 shallots, sliced

450 g/1 lb sliced button mushrooms

1 tsp plain flour

150 ml/5 fl oz double cream

2 tbsp port

115 g/4 oz sun-dried tomatoes, chopped

freshly grated nutmeg

450g /1 lb dried spaghetti

1 tbsp freshly chopped parsley

salt and pepper

triangles of fried white bread, to serve

1 Heat the butter and 1 tablespoon of the oil in a large pan. Add the sliced shallots and cook over a medium heat for 3 minutes. Add the mushrooms and cook over a low heat for 2 minutes. Season with salt and pepper, sprinkle over the flour and cook, stirring constantly, for 1 minute.

2 Gradually stir in the cream and port, add the sun-dried tomatoes and a pinch of grated nutmeg, and cook over a low heat for 8 minutes.

3 Meanwhile, bring a large saucepan of lightly salted water to the boil. Add the spaghetti and remaining olive oil and cook for 12–14 minutes, or until tender but still firm to the bite.

4 Drain the spaghetti and return to the pan. Pour over the mushroom sauce and cook for 3 minutes. Transfer the spaghetti to a large serving plate and sprinkle over the chopped parsley. Serve with crispy triangles of fried bread.

## VARIATION

Non-vegetarians could add 115 g/4 oz Parma ham, cut into thin strips and heated gently in 2 tablespoons of butter, to the pasta, along with the mushroom sauce.

# Walnut and Olive Fettuccine

This mouth-watering dish would make an excellent light, vegetarian lunch for four, or a good starter for six.

## NUTRITIONAL INFORMATION

| | | | |
|---|---|---|---|
| Calories | 804 | Sugars | 5g |
| Protein | 19g | Fat | 65g |
| Carbohydrate | 34g | Saturates | 15g |

10 mins    5 mins

### SERVES 4–6

## I N G R E D I E N T S

2 thick slices wholemeal bread,
  crusts removed

300 ml/10 fl oz milk

275 g/9½ oz shelled walnuts

2 garlic cloves, crushed

115 g/4 oz stoned black olives

60 g/2 oz freshly grated Parmesan cheese

125 ml/4 fl oz extra virgin olive oil

150 ml/5 fl oz double cream

450 g/1 lb fresh fettuccine

salt and pepper

2–3 tbsp chopped fresh parsley

4 Bring a large pan of lightly salted water to the boil. Add the fettuccine and half of the remaining oil and cook for 2–3 minutes, or until tender, but still firm to the bite. Drain thoroughly, and toss with the remaining olive oil.

5 Divide the cooked fettuccine between individual serving plates and spoon the olive, garlic and walnut sauce on top. Sprinkle over the fresh parsley and serve.

1 Put the bread in a shallow dish, pour over the milk and set aside to soak until the liquid has been absorbed.

2 Spread the walnuts out on a baking tray and toast in a preheated oven, 190°C/375°F/Gas Mark 5, for 5 minutes, until golden. Set aside to cool.

3 Put the soaked bread, walnuts, garlic, black olives, Parmesan cheese and 6 tablespoons of the olive oil in a food processor and blend to a purée. Season to taste and stir in the cream.

# Pasta & Vegetable Sauce

The shapes and textures of the vegetables make a mouthwatering presentation in this light and summery dish.

## NUTRITIONAL INFORMATION

Calories ...... 389   Sugars ........ 4g
Protein ....... 16g   Fat .......... 20g
Carbohydrate .. 38g   Saturates ..... 11g

 10 mins    30 mins

### SERVES 4

## I N G R E D I E N T S

225 g/8 oz dried gemelli or other
    pasta shapes

1 tbsp olive oil

1 head green broccoli, cut into florets

2 courgettes, sliced

225 g/8 oz asparagus spears

115 g/4 oz mangetouts

115 g/4 oz frozen peas

2 tbsp butter

3 tbsp vegetable stock

4 tbsp double cream

freshly grated nutmeg

2 tbsp chopped fresh parsley

2 tbsp freshly grated Parmesan cheese

salt and pepper

1 Bring a large saucepan of lightly salted water to the boil. Add the pasta and olive oil and cook for 8–10 minutes, or until tender, but still firm to the bite. Drain, return to the pan, cover and keep warm.

2 Steam the broccoli, courgettes, asparagus spears and mangetouts over a pan of boiling salted water until they are just beginning to soften. Remove from the heat and refresh in cold water. Drain thoroughly and set aside.

3 Bring a small pan of lightly salted water to the boil. Add the frozen peas and cook for 3 minutes. Drain the peas, refresh in cold water and then drain again. Set aside with the other vegetables.

4 Put the butter and vegetable stock in a pan over a medium heat. Add all of the vegetables, reserving a few of the asparagus spears, and toss carefully with a wooden spoon until they have heated through, taking care not to break them up.

5 Stir in the cream and heat through without bringing to the boil. Season to taste with salt, pepper and nutmeg.

6 Transfer the pasta to a warmed serving dish and stir in the chopped parsley. Spoon over the vegetable sauce and sprinkle over the Parmesan cheese. Arrange the reserved asparagus spears in a pattern on top and serve.

# Filled Aubergines

Combined with tomatoes and melting mozzarella cheese, pasta makes a tasty filling for baked aubergine shells.

## NUTRITIONAL INFORMATION

| | |
|---|---|
| Calories . . . . . . 342 | Sugars . . . . . . . . 6g |
| Protein . . . . . . . 11g | Fat . . . . . . . . . . 16g |
| Carbohydrate . . 40g | Saturates . . . . . . 4g |

25 mins          55 mins

### SERVES 4

## INGREDIENTS

225 g/8 oz dried penne or other short
   pasta shapes

4 tbsp olive oil, plus extra for brushing

2 aubergines

1 large onion, chopped

2 garlic cloves, crushed

400 g/14 oz canned chopped tomatoes

2 tsp dried oregano

55 g/2 oz mozzarella cheese, thinly sliced

25 g/1 oz freshly grated Parmesan cheese

2 tbsp dry breadcrumbs

salt and pepper

salad leaves, to serve

1 Bring a large saucepan of lightly salted water to the boil. Add the pasta and 1 tablespoon of the olive oil, bring back to the boil and cook for 8–10 minutes, or until tender, but still firm to the bite. Drain, return to the pan, cover and keep warm.

2 Cut the aubergines in half lengthways and score around the inside with a sharp knife, being careful not to pierce the shells. Scoop out the flesh with a spoon. Brush the insides of the shells with olive oil. Chop the flesh and set aside.

3 Heat the remaining oil in a frying pan. Fry the onion until translucent. Add the garlic and fry for 1 minute. Add the chopped aubergine and fry, stirring frequently, for 5 minutes.

4 Add the chopped tomatoes and the oregano to the pan, and season to taste with salt and pepper. Bring the mixture to the boil and simmer for 10 minutes, or until it has thickened. Remove the pan from the heat and stir in the pasta carefully using a wooden spoon.

5 Brush a baking tray with oil and arrange the aubergine shells in one layer. Divide half the tomato and pasta between them. Scatter mozzarella slices over the mixture and pile the remaining tomato and pasta mixture on top. Mix the Parmesan and breadcrumbs and sprinkle over, patting it lightly into the mixture.

6 Bake in a preheated oven, 200°C/ 400°F/Gas Mark 6, for 25 minutes or until the topping is golden brown. Serve hot with a selection of mixed salad leaves.

# Lemon-flavoured Spaghetti

Steaming vegetables helps to preserve their nutritional content, and allows them to retain their bright, natural colours and crunchy texture.

## NUTRITIONAL INFORMATION

| | | |
|---|---|---|
| Calories | ...... 133 | Sugars ........ 8g |
| Protein | ........ 8g | Fat ........... 1g |
| Carbohydrate | .. 25g | Saturates .... 0.2g |

 10 mins    25 mins

### SERVES 4

## INGREDIENTS

225 g/8 oz celeriac

2 medium carrots

2 medium leeks

1 small red pepper

1 small yellow pepper

2 garlic cloves

1 tsp celery seeds

1 tbsp lemon juice

300 g/10½ oz spaghetti

chopped celery leaves, to garnish

### LEMON DRESSING

1 tsp finely grated lemon rind

1 tbsp lemon juice

4 tbsp low-fat natural fromage frais

salt and pepper

2 tbsp snipped fresh chives

1 Peel the celeriac and carrots, cut into thin matchsticks and place in a bowl. Trim and slice the leeks, rinse under running water to flush out any dirt, then shred finely. Halve, deseed and slice the peppers. Peel and thinly slice the garlic.

2 Add all of the vegetables to the bowl with the celeriac and the carrots. Toss the vegetables with the celery seeds and lemon juice.

3 Bring a large saucepan of water to the boil and cook the spaghetti according to the instructions on the packet. Drain and keep warm.

4 Meanwhile, bring another large saucepan of water to the boil, put the vegetables in a steamer or sieve and place over the boiling water. Cover and steam for 6–7 minutes, or until the vegetables are just tender.

5 While the spaghetti and vegetables are cooking, mix the ingredients for the lemon dressing together.

6 Transfer the spaghetti and vegetables to a warm serving bowl and mix with the dressing. Garnish with chopped celery leaves and serve.

# Pesto Pasta

Italian pesto is usually laden with fat. This version has just as much flavour but is much healthier.

## NUTRITIONAL INFORMATION

Calories ...... 283  Sugars ........ 5g
Protein ....... 14g  Fat ........... 3g
Carbohydrate .. 37g  Saturates ...... 1g

 1 hr       30 mins

### SERVES 4

## I N G R E D I E N T S

225 g/8 oz chestnut mushrooms, sliced

150 ml/5 fl oz fresh vegetable stock

175 g/6 oz asparagus, trimmed and cut into 5 cm/2 inch lengths

300 g/10½ oz green and white tagliatelle

400 g/14 oz canned artichoke hearts, drained and halved

grissini (bread sticks), to serve

### P E S T O   S A U C E

2 large garlic cloves, crushed

15 g/½ oz fresh basil leaves, washed

6 tbsp low-fat natural fromage frais

2 tbsp freshly grated Parmesan cheese

salt and pepper

### T O   G A R N I S H

basil leaves, shredded

Parmesan shavings

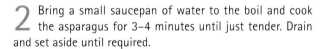

1 Place the mushrooms in a saucepan with the stock. Bring to the boil, cover and simmer for 3–4 minutes until just tender. Drain and set aside, reserving the liquor to use in soups if wished.

2 Bring a small saucepan of water to the boil and cook the asparagus for 3–4 minutes until just tender. Drain and set aside until required.

3 Bring a large pan of lightly salted water to the boil and cook the tagliatelle according to the instructions on the packet. Drain, return to the pan and keep warm.

4 Meanwhile, make the pesto sauce. Place all of the ingredients in a blender or food processor and process for a few seconds until smooth. Alternatively, finely chop the basil and mix all the ingredients together.

5 Add the artichoke hearts and cooked mushrooms and asparagus to the pasta and cook, stirring, over a low heat for 2–3 minutes.

6 Remove the pasta and vegetable mixture from the heat and mix in the pesto. Stir well to mix.

7 Transfer to a warm bowl. Garnish with shredded basil leaves and Parmesan shavings and serve with grissini.

# Pasta & Herring Salad

This salad, which so many countries claim as their own, is considered in Holland to be a typically Dutch dish.

## NUTRITIONAL INFORMATION

| | | |
|---|---|---|
| Calories ......774 | Sugars .......21g |
| Protein .......33g | Fat ..........31g |
| Carbohydrate ..97g | Saturates ......4g |

1½ hrs    15 mins

### SERVES 4

## INGREDIENTS

250 g/9 oz dried pasta shells

5 tbsp olive oil

400 g/14 oz rollmop herrings in brine

6 boiled potatoes

2 large tart apples

2 baby frisée lettuces

2 baby beetroot

4 hard-boiled eggs

6 pickled onions

6 pickled gherkins

2 tbsp capers

3 tbsp of tarragon vinegar

salt and pepper

 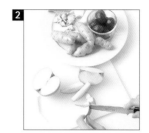 

## VARIATION

This recipe also works well with wholemeal pasta, which complements the richness of the fish.

1 Bring a large saucepan of lightly salted water to the boil. Add the pasta and 1 tablespoon of the olive oil, and cook until tender but still firm to the bite. Drain the pasta and refresh in cold water.

2 Cut the herrings, potatoes, apples, frisée lettuces and beetroot into small pieces. Put all of these ingredients into a large salad bowl.

3 Drain the pasta thoroughly and add to the salad bowl. Toss lightly to mix the pasta and herring mixture together. Season.

4 Carefully shell the hard-boiled eggs, then slice. Garnish the salad with the slices of egg, pickled onions, pickled gherkins and capers, sprinkle with the remaining olive oil and the tarragon vinegar, season to taste and serve immediately.

# Cheese, Nut & Pasta Salad

Use colourful salad leaves to provide visual contrast to match the contrasts of taste and texture.

## NUTRITIONAL INFORMATION

| | | | |
|---|---|---|---|
| Calories | ...... 694 | Sugars | ........ 1g |
| Protein | ....... 22g | Fat | .......... 57g |
| Carbohydrate | .. 24g | Saturates | ..... 15g |

 15 mins  15–20 mins

### SERVES 4

## INGREDIENTS

225 g/8 oz dried pasta shells

1 tbsp olive oil

115 g/4 oz shelled and halved walnuts

mixed salad leaves, such as radicchio,
escarole, rocket, lamb's lettuce and frisée

225 g/8 oz dolcelatte cheese, crumbled

salt

### DRESSING

2 tbsp walnut oil

4 tbsp extra virgin olive oil

2 tbsp red wine vinegar

salt and pepper

1 Boil a large pan of lightly salted water. Add the pasta shells and olive oil and cook for 8–10 minutes or until tender but al diente. Drain the pasta, refresh under cold running water, drain again, and set aside.

2 Spread out the shelled walnut halves onto a baking tray and toast under a preheated grill for 2–3 minutes. Set aside to cool while you make the dressing.

3 To make the dressing, whisk together the walnut oil, olive oil and vinegar in a small bowl, and season to taste.

4 To make up the salad arrange the salad leaves in a large serving bowl. Pile the cooled pasta in the middle of the salad leaves and sprinkle over them the dolcelatte cheese. Just before serving, pour the dressing over the pasta salad, scatter the walnut halves on top, and toss together to coat with dressing. Serve immediately.

## COOK'S TIP

Dolcelatte is a semi-soft, blue-veined cheese from Italy. Its texture is creamy and smooth and the flavour is delicate, but piquant. You could use Roquefort instead. It is essential that whatever cheese you choose, it is of the best quality and in peak condition.

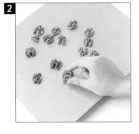

# Goat's Cheese & Penne Salad

This superb salad is delicious when served with strongly flavoured meat dishes, such as venison.

## NUTRITIONAL INFORMATION

| | | | |
|---|---|---|---|
| Calories | 634 | Sugars | 13g |
| Protein | 18g | Fat | 51g |
| Carbohydrate | 27g | Saturates | 13g |

1 hr 5 mins    10 mins

### SERVES 4

## INGREDIENTS

250 g/9 oz dried penne

5 tbsp olive oil

1 head radicchio, torn into pieces

1 Webbs lettuce, torn into pieces

90 g/3¼ oz chopped walnuts

2 ripe pears, cored and diced

1 fresh basil sprig

1 bunch of watercress, trimmed or young spinach leaves, coarsely chopped

2 tbsp lemon juice

3 tbsp garlic vinegar

4 tomatoes, quartered

1 small onion, sliced

1 large carrot, grated

250 g/9 oz goat's cheese, diced

salt and pepper

1 Bring a large saucepan of lightly salted water to the boil. Add the penne and 1 tablespoon of the olive oil and cook for 8–10 minutes, or until tender, but still firm to the bite. Drain the pasta, refresh under cold running water, drain thoroughly again and set aside to cool.

2 Place the radicchio and Webbs lettuce in a large salad bowl and mix together well. Top with the pasta, walnuts, pears, basil and watercress or spinach.

3 Mix together the lemon juice, the remaining olive oil and the vinegar in a measuring jug. Pour the mixture over the salad ingredients and toss to coat the salad leaves well.

4 Add the tomato quarters, onion slices, grated carrot and diced goat's cheese to the salad and toss together, using 2 forks, until well mixed. Leave the salad to chill in the refrigerator for about 1 hour before serving.

## COOK'S TIP

Radicchio is a variety of chicory which originated in Italy. It has a slightly bitter flavour.

# Pasta & Garlic Mayo Salad

This crisp salad would make an excellent accompaniment to grilled meat and is ideal for summer barbecues.

## NUTRITIONAL INFORMATION

Calories ...... 858  Sugars ....... 35g
Protein ....... 11g  Fat .......... 64g
Carbohydrate .. 64g  Saturates ...... 8g

1½ hrs     10 mins

### SERVES 4

## I N G R E D I E N T S

2 large lettuces

250 g/9 oz dried penne

1 tbsp olive oil

8 red eating apples

juice of 4 lemons

1 head of celery, sliced

115 g/4 oz shelled, halved walnuts

250 ml/9 fl oz fresh garlic mayonnaise (see Cook's Tip)

salt

1 Wash, drain and pat dry the lettuce leaves with kitchen paper. Refrigerate for 1 hour or until crisp.

2 Meanwhile, bring a large pan of lightly salted water to the boil. Add the pasta and olive oil and cook for 8–10 minutes, or until it is tender, but still al diente - firm to the bite. Drain, then refresh under cold running water. Drain thoroughly again and set aside.

3 Core and dice the apples, place them in a bowl and sprinkle with lemon juice.

4 Mix together the pasta, celery, apples and walnuts and toss in the garlic mayonnaise (see Cook's Tip, below).

5 Line a salad bowl with the lettuce leaves and spoon the pasta salad into the lined bowl before serving.

## COOK'S TIP

For garlic mayo, beat 2 egg yolks with a pinch of salt and 6 crushed garlic cloves. Beat in 350ml/ 12 fl oz oil, 1–2 teaspoons at a time. When ¼ of the oil has been incorporated, beat in 1–2 tablespoons white wine vinegar. Continue beating in the oil. Stir in 1 teaspoon Dijon mustard and season.

# Italian Fusilli Salad

Tomatoes and mozzarella cheese are a classic Italian combination. Here they are joined with pasta spirals and avocado for a touch of luxury.

## NUTRITIONAL INFORMATION

| | | | |
|---|---|---|---|
| Calories | ...... 660 | Sugars | ........ 7g |
| Protein | ....... 22g | Fat | .......... 47g |
| Carbohydrate | .. 39g | Saturates | ..... 13g |

15 mins     10 mins

### SERVES 4

## INGREDIENTS

2 tbsp pine kernels

175 g/6 oz dried fusilli

1 tbsp olive oil

6 tomatoes

225 g/8 oz mozzarella cheese

1 large avocado pear

2 tbsp lemon juice

3 tbsp chopped fresh basil

salt and pepper

fresh basil sprigs, to garnish

### DRESSING

6 tbsp extra virgin olive oil

2 tbsp white wine vinegar

1 tsp wholegrain mustard

pinch of sugar

1 Spread the pine kernels out on a baking tray and toast under a preheated grill for 1–2 minutes until golden. Remove and set aside to cool.

2 Bring a large saucepan of lightly salted water to the boil. Add the fusilli and olive oil and cook until tender, but still firm to the bite. Drain the pasta thoroughly and refresh in cold water. Drain again and set aside to cool.

3 Thinly slice the tomatoes and the mozzarella cheese.

4 Cut the avocado pear in half and remove the stone and skin. Cut into thin slices lengthways and sprinkle with lemon juice to prevent discoloration.

5 To make the dressing, whisk together the oil, vinegar, mustard and sugar in a small bowl, and season to taste with salt and black pepper.

6 Arrange the tomato, mozzarella and avocado slices alternately, overlapping one another, on a large serving platter.

7 Toss the cooled pasta with half of the dressing and the chopped basil and season to taste with salt and black pepper. Spoon the pasta into the centre of the serving platter and pour over the remaining dressing. Sprinkle over the toasted pine kernels, garnish with fresh basil sprigs and serve immediately.

# Spicy Sausage Salad

A warm sausage and pasta dressing spooned over chilled salad leaves makes a refreshing combination to start a meal.

## NUTRITIONAL INFORMATION

Calories ...... 383   Sugars ........ 2g
Protein ....... 11g   Fat .......... 28g
Carbohydrate .. 20g   Saturates ...... 1g

15 mins    25 mins

### SERVES 4

## I N G R E D I E N T S

125g/4½ oz small pasta shapes, such as elbow tubetti

3 tbsp olive oil

1 medium onion, chopped

2 cloves garlic, crushed

1 small yellow pepper, cored, deseeded and cut into matchsticks

175 g/6 oz spicy pork sausage such as chorizo, Italian pepperoni or salami, skinned and sliced

2 tbsp red wine

1 tbsp red wine vinegar

mixed salad leaves, chilled

salt

1 Cook the pasta in a pan of boiling salted water, adding 1 tablespoon of the olive oil, for 8–10 minutes, or until tender. Drain in a colander and set aside.

2 Heat the remaining oil in a saucepan over a medium heat. Fry the onion until it is translucent, stir in the garlic, yellow pepper and sliced sausage and cook for 3–4 minutes, stirring once or twice.

3 Add the wine, wine vinegar and reserved pasta to the pan, stir to blend well and bring the mixture just to the boil.

4 Arrange the chilled salad leaves on individual serving plates, spoon on the warm sausage and pasta mixture, and serve immediately.

## VARIATION

Other suitable sausages include the Italian pepperoni, flavoured with chilli peppers, fennel and spices, and one of the many varieties of salami, usually flavoured with garlic and pepper.

This is a Parragon Book
This edition published in 2002

Parragon
Queen Street House
4 Queen Street
Bath BA1 1HE, UK

ISBN: 0-75257-538-4

Printed in China

**NOTE**

This book uses metric and imperial measurements. Follow the same units
of measurement throughout; do not mix metric and imperial.
All spoon measurements are level: teaspoons are assumed to be 5 ml, and
tablespoons are assumed to be 15 ml. Unless otherwise stated,
milk is assumed to be full fat, eggs and individual vegetables such as potatoes
are medium, and pepper is freshly ground black pepper.

The nutritional information provided for each recipe is per serving or per person.
Optional ingredients, variations or serving suggestions have
not been included in the calculations. The times given for each recipe are an approximate
guide only because the preparation times may differ according to the techniques used by
different people and the cooking times may vary as a result of the type of oven used.

Recipes using raw or very lightly cooked eggs should be
avoided by infants, the elderly, pregnant women, convalescents,
and anyone suffering from an illness.

*The publisher would like to thank
Steamer Trading Cookshop, Lewes, East Sussex, for the kind loan of props.*